Picnic & Barbecue Menus

Great Meals in Minutes was created by Rebus Inc., and
published by Time-Life Books.

This edition published 1994 by Bloomsbury Books, an
imprint of The Godfrey Cave Group, 42 Bloomsbury Street,
London, WC1B 3QJ.

© 1994 Time-Life Books BV.

ISBN 1 85471 586 0

Printed and bound in Great Britain.

Picnic & Barbecue Menus

Jane Uetz

Menu 1
Oriental Chicken and Rice Salad   8
Chinese Cabbage, Snow Peas, Cucumber with Mayonnaise
Pineapple with Orange-Chocolate Sauce

Menu 2
Butterflied Leg of Lamb with Savoury Sauce   10
Stir-Fried Courgette and Yellow Squash
Fresh Mint and Watercress Salad

Menu 3
Monterey Beef Roast   12
Roast Potatoes with Herbed Butter
Carrot and Broccoli Salad

Roberta Rall

Menu 1
Grilled Poussins with Oriental Flavours   16
Stir-Fried Carrots with Snow Peas
Fresh Fruit in Cookie Cups

Menu 2
Grilled Monkfish with Lime-Butter Baste   18
Marinated Vegetables
Bulgur with Carrots and Scallions

Menu 3
Great Grilled Burgers   20
Raw Vegetables with Creamy Basil Dip
Fruit Layers with Vanilla Sauce

Ron Davis

Menu 1
Duck, Chicken, and Veal Salad   24
Pasta with Three Cheeses
Asparagus with Garlic Dressing

Menu 2
Grilled Trout with Spinach, Bread, and Vegetable Stuffing   26
Tomato, Onion, and Watercress Salad
Leeks with Roasted Pepper and Bucheron Cheese

Menu 3
Scallop Seviche   30
Sweet-and-Spicy Barbecued Spareribs
Honey-Mustard Coleslaw

Victoria Wise

Menu 1
Salmon Barbecued with Fennel, Lemon, and Onion   36
Grilled Corn
Cucumbers and Radishes with Watercress

Menu 2
Grilled Rabbit   38
Grilled Yellow and Green Bell Peppers
Mediterranean Tomato Salad

Menu 3
Pork Loin Roasted with Garlic and Sage   40
Artichokes Oreganata
Tapénade

Bruce Cliborne

Menu 1
Grilled Clams, Oysters, and Lobsters   44
Herbed New Potatoes, Carrots, and Scallions
Cucumbers and Tomatoes with Lime

Menu 2
Grilled Loin of Pork with Fresh Thyme   46
Marinated Corn Salad
Sweet-and-Sour Peaches and Plums

Menu 3
Sea Scallops with Herbed Crème Fraîche   50
Poached Fennel
Orange, Radish, and Coriander Salad

Nicholas Baxter

Menu 1
Loin of Lamb with Tomato and Mushroom Stuffing   54
Watercress and Hazelnut Salad
Pasta with Sour Cream and Black Pepper

Menu 2
Grilled Salmon Steaks with Fresh Dill and Thyme   56
Mélange of French Vegetables

Menu 3
Loin of Veal Poached with Vegetables in White Wine   59
Wild Rice with Red Pepper and Cassis

Bloomsbury Books
London

Jane Uetz

Menu 1
(left)
Oriental Chicken and Rice Salad
Chinese Cabbage, Snow Peas, and
Cucumber with Curried Mayonnaise
Pineapple with Orange-Chocolate Sauce

When planning her meals, whether formal or informal, Jane Uetz likes to inject a surprise element, a special touch that elicits comments from her guests. This could mean a simple meal with a spectacular dessert or one with an exotic appetizer. An example of her approach is Menu 2 in which she features a grilled butterflied leg of lamb, a sumptuous and distinctive cut of meat that has marinated in a flavourful piquant sauce. In Menu 3, the main course is an unusual beef roast that is coated with mustard and salt, then placed directly onto hot coals for grilling.

Her style of cooking is light, fresh, and uncomplicated. She willingly experiments with flavours and may combine several cuisines in one meal. For the picnic in Menu 1, she offers an Oriental salad consisting of chicken breasts cut into strips and combined with chilled rice, red pepper, and scallions. Although the green salad calls for two Chinese vegetables, she seasons them with Indian curry-flavoured mayonnaise. And her dessert has French overtones – fresh pineapple served with an orange-chocolate sauce.

Note: All tablespoon measurements in these recipes are level tablespoons, unless otherwise stated.

A wicker basket lined with bandannas contains a picnic in three separate bowls: chicken and rice salad; cabbage, snowpea, and cucumber salad; and chunks of fresh pineapple with orange-choclate sauce on the side.

Oriental Chicken and Rice Salad
Chinese Cabbage, Snow Peas, and Cucumber with Curried Mayonnaise
Pineapple with Orange-Chocolate Sauce

This picnic consists of two substantial main-course salads, one of meat and one of vegetables, and a refreshing pineapple dessert. The vegetable salad calls for Chinese cabbage, also known as Napa or celery cabbage, a variety with a long head. Its broad leaves are crinkly and tender, and often fringed with pale green. Chinese cabbage has a fresh, delicate noncabbagey flavour.

Chinese pea pods, or snow peas, are another component of this salad. These edible pods are sweet, crisp, and delicious raw. Select unblemished, firm green pods and refrigerate them in a plastic bag. Sugar snap peas make good substitutes.

Carry the chocolate sauce for the pinapple in a small Thermos® container, or pour it hot into a jar and wrap the jar in a towel.

What to drink
Serve cold beer, light ale, or a fruity, cold white wine. Italian Pinot Grigio or Pinot Bianco would be excellent choices, as would a French Muscadet.

Start-to-Finish Steps
1 Follow chicken salad recipe steps 1 through 3.
2 While chicken is poaching, grate ginger and coarsely chop nuts for salad recipe. Halve cabbage lengthwise and follow cabbage recipe step 1.
3 Follow chicken recipe steps 4 and 5.
4 While chicken and rice are cooling, follow cabbage recipe steps 2 through 4, and pineapple recipe steps 1 and 2.
5 Follow chicken recipe steps 6 through 11 and cabbage recipe step 5.
6 Follow pineapple recipe steps 3 and 4, and pack picnic if transporting.
7 Follow chicken recipe step 12, cabbage recipe step 6, and serve.
8 For dessert, follow pineapple recipe step 5 and serve.

Oriental Chicken and Rice Salad

½ teaspoon salt
150 g (5 oz) long-grain rice
375 ml (13 fl oz) chicken stock
2 whole chicken breasts, skinned and boned (about 500 g (1 lb) total weight)
Small red bell pepper
3 scallions
60 ml (2 fl oz) cold-pressed sesame oil
3 tablespoons soy sauce
2 tablespoons dry sherry
1 teaspoon freshly grated ginger
¼ teaspoon hot pepper sauce
60 g (2 oz) coarsely chopped pecans, unsalted peanuts, or cashews

1 In a medium-size saucepan, combine ½ teaspoon salt and 350 ml (12 fl oz) water. Cover and bring to a boil over medium-high heat.
2 Add rice to boiling water, stir once with fork, and reduce heat to a gentle simmer. Cover pan and cook exactly 18 minutes.
3 While rice is cooking, bring stock to a boil in another medium-size saucepan over medium-high heat. Add chicken breasts, reduce heat to a gentle simmer, and poach breasts 10 to 15 minutes, or until a knife inserted in the centre of the chicken breasts reveal rosy white flesh.
4 With slotted spoon, transfer chicken breasts to cutting board or counter. Let breasts cool slightly, about 15 minutes.
5 Remove rice from heat, fluff lightly with fork, and spread out on platter to cool, about 15 minutes.
6 Wash red pepper and pat dry with paper towels. Core, halve, and seed pepper. Cut into slivers.
7 Wash scallions and pat dry with paper towels. With chef's knife, trim off ends and cut into 1-inch lengths.
8 With chef's knife, cut cooled chicken breasts into 5 mm (¼ inch) strips.
9 In medium-size bowl, combine red pepper, scallions, chicken strips, and cooled rice, and toss gently with fork to combine.
10 In small bowl, combine sesame oil, soy sauce,

sherry, ginger, and hot pepper sauce. Pour over salad and toss with fork until evenly coated.

11 Cover salad with plastic wrap and chill until ready to leave for picnic or to serve.

12 Just before serving, add nuts and toss with fork to combine.

Chinese Cabbage, Snow Peas, and Cucumber with Curried Mayonnaise

$^1/_2$ small head Chinese cabbage
125 g (4 oz) snow peas
Small cucumber
4 tablespoons mayonnaise
1 tablespoon vegetable oil
1 tablespoon white wine vinegar
1 teaspoon curry powder

1 Peel off any damaged outer leaves from cabbage and discard. With chef's knife, cut cabbage crosswise into $2^1/_2$ cm (1 inch) wide pieces. In colander, wash and drain cabbage. Dry in salad spinner or pat dry with paper towels and transfer to salad bowl.

2 Trim and string snow peas. Wash under cold water and pat dry with paper towels. With chef's knife, cut snow peas lengthwise into julienne strips. Add to salad bowl.

3 With vegetable peeler or paring knife, peel cucumber. Halve cucumber lengthwise and, with teaspoon, scoop out seeds. Lay each half cut side

down and cut into1 cm ($^1/_2$ inch) thick slices. Add to salad bowl.

4 With salad servers, toss salad ingredients to combine. Cover bowl with plastic wrap, and chill at least 15 minutes or until ready to leave for picnic or to serve.

5 For dressing, combine remaining ingredients in small bowl and whisk until blended. Transfer to small jar with lid and refrigerate until ready to leave for picnic or to serve. If transporting in hot weather, be sure to pack dressing in ice chest.

6 Just before serving, spoon dressing over salad and, with salad servers, toss to coat.

Pineapple with Orange-Chocolate Sauce

Medium-size pineapple (about 1.75 Kg ($3^1/_2$ lb))
60 g (2 oz) unsweetened chocolate, broken into pieces
60 g (2 oz) semisweet chocolate bits
1 tablespoon unsalted butter
60 g (2 oz) sugar
125 ml (4 fl oz) orange liqueur

1 With chef's knife, cut $^3/_4$-inch-thick slice from top and bottom of pinapple and discard.

2 Pare pineapple, starting from top and following contours of pineapple with knife. With tip of paring knife or vegetable peeler, remove eyes. Cutting from top to bottom, cut pineapple into $1–1^1/_2$ cm ($^1/_2$-$^3/_4$ inch) thick slices. Halve each slice crosswise and cut out core. Cut slices into fingers, about $2^1/_2$ cm by 10 cm (1 inch by 4 inches). Arrange on platter, cover loosely with plastic wrap, and chill at least 20 minutes or until ready to serve.

3 In top of double boiler, combine unsweetened chocolate, chocolate bits, and butter. In bottom of double boiler, bring about $2^1/_2$ cm (1 inch) of water to a boil. Reduce heat to a simmer and set top of double boiler into bottom. Heat mixture, stirring occasionally, until chocolate melts, about 3 minutes.

4 With whisk, stir mixture until well blended. Still stirring, add sugar and orange liqueur, and cook, stirring constantly, until sauce is thick and smooth and sugar has melted, 4 to 5 minutes. Transfer to Thermos® or to jar. If using jar, wrap immediately in towel to keep warm

5 Just before serving, stir sauce to recombine, if necessary, and spoon it into small Chinese teacups or other small bowls for dipping.

9

Butterflied Leg of Lamb with Savoury Sauce
Stir-Fried Courgette and Yellow Squash
Fresh Mint and Watercress Salad

To serve this barbecue, lay out decorative placemats for your diners. Arrange the lamb slices topped with sauce and the stir-fried squash on individual plates and serve the watercress salad separately.

To organize this barbecue properly, prepare the salad while the lamb is grilling. When the lamb is done, let it rest off the fire while you stir-fry the courgette and yellow squash and toss the salad at the very last moment.

To butterfly a leg of lamb means to debone the meat, leaving one large flat piece with a butterfly shape. Unless you are skilled at carving, ask your butcher to do this. This cut of lamb is delicious barbecued, but because it is not uniformly thick, some portions of the meat will cook more quickly than others.

What to drink
The best accompaniment to this meal is a fruity young Zinfandel or a Beaujolais. A good beer or ale would also be appropriate.

Start-to-Finish Steps

Thirty minutes ahead: Start barbecue and bring lamb to room temperature.

1 Follow lamb recipe steps 1 through 3.
2 While lamb is grilling, peel and finely mince onion for lamb and squash recipes.
3 Follow salad recipe steps 1 through 3.
4 Follow lamb recipe steps 4 and 5.
5 While lamb is grilling, wash, dry, and chop fresh basil, if using, and follow squash recipe steps 1 and 2.
6 Follow lamb recipe step 6.
7 While lamb is resting, follow squash recipe steps 3 through 5.
8 Follow salad recipe step 4, lamb recipe step 7, and serve with squash.

Butterflied Leg of Lamb with Savoury Sauce

1 clove garlic
2 Kg (4 lb) leg of lamb, boned and butterflied, at room temperature
Salt and freshly ground pepper
4 tablespoons unsalted butter
3 tablespoons cider vinegar

3 tablespoons ketchup
2 tablespoons dark brown sugar
1 tablespoon dry mustard
1 tablespoon Worcestershire sauce
1 tablespoon finely minced onion
1 bay leaf
1/2 teaspoon paprika
1/4 teaspoon hot pepper sauce

1 Peel garlic and cut into slivers.
2 With paring knife, make several 2–2 1/2 cm (3/4–1 inch) slits in the lamb and, with your fingers, insert a garlic sliver in each of the slits. Sprinkle lamb with salt and pepper to taste and pat meat to make seasoning adhere.
3 Place meat on grill, fat side down, 10–15 cm (4–6 inches) from source of heat. Grill 15 minutes for rare and 20 minutes for medium.
4 With long-handled double-pronged fork, turn lamb, and grill 15 to 20 minutes more, or until outside is crusty brown and interior has reached desired degree of doneness.
5 In small saucepan set on burner or side of barbecue grill, melt butter. Add 4 tbsps water, 1 teaspoon salt, and remaining ingredients, and stir with fork until blended. Cook mixture, uncovered, stirring occasionally, over medium-low heat 20 minutes.
6 Transfer lamb to cutting board and allow meat to rest 10 minutes before slicing. Cover sauce and keep warm until ready to serve.
7 Cut meat into 1 cm (1/2 inch) slices and top with warm sauce.

Stir-Fried Courgette and Yellow Squash

1/2 clove garlic
Small courgette
Small yellow squash
2 tablespoons unsalted butter
Medium-size onion, peeled and minced
1 tablespoon chopped fresh basil, or 1 teaspoon dried
Salt and freshly ground pepper

1 Peel and mince garlic.
2 Wash courgette and yellow squash, and pat dry with paper towels. With chef's knife, cut into 5 mm (1/4 inch) thick slices.
3 In large skillet, melt butter over medium-high heat. Add garlic and onion and, stirring with wooden spoon, stir fry until onion is barely crisp-tender, 2 to 3 minutes.
4 Add courgette, yellow squash, and basil, and stir

fry another 2 to 3 minutes, or until squash is crisp-tender.
5 Remove pan from heat, season with salt and pepper to taste, and stir to blend. Keep mixture warm over very low heat until ready to serve.

Fresh Mint and Watercress Salad

2 bunches watercress
60 g (2 oz) whole, fresh mint leaves, or 2 teaspoons dried
2 tablespoons walnut oil
1 tablespoon safflower oil
1 tablespoon red wine vinegar
Salt and freshly ground pepper

1 In colander, wash watercress and fresh mint, if using, and dry in salad spinner or pat dry with paper towels. Remove stems and discard.
2 In salad bowl, combine watercress and mint leaves. Cover with plastic wrap and refrigerate until ready to serve.
3 In small bowl, combine walnut and safflower oils, vinegar, dried mint leaves, if not using fresh, and salt and pepper to taste. With fork, beat until blended. Set aside.
4 Just before serving, stir dressing to recombine and pour over salad. With salad servers, toss greens until lightly coated. Divide among individual plates or bowls.

Leftover suggestion
Leftover lamb can be julienned and added to stir-fried vegetables for a simple main dish. Or, it may be sliced and served cold on a vegetable platter with a light vinaigrette.

Monterey Beef Roast
Roast Potatoes with Herbed Butter
Carrot and Broccoli Salad

For this barbecue, both the beef roast and the potatoes are grilled simultaneously, so prepare your salad while they are cooking.

The beef roast for this barbecue is a dish Jane Uetz discovered in California many years ago. The beef is covered with mustard, coated completely with a crust of coarse salt, then laid directly on a bed of hot coals. The salt coating will turn black as the meat sears, sealing in the juices.

What to drink
The beef roast calls for a robust red wine. First choice would be a Californian Zinfandel; second, but equally good, would be a Rhône wine like Châteauneuf-du-Pape.

Start-to-Finish Steps

Thirty minutes ahead: Start barbecue: Prepare a bed of coals 5–7.5 cm (2–3 inches) deep.

1 Follow potatoes recipe steps 1 through 3 and roast recipe steps 1 through 3. (To calculate when to start beef roast, subtract desired cooking time plus 10-minute resting time from time at which potatoes will be done.)
2 While beef is cooking, follow salad recipe steps 1 through 12 and potatoes recipe step 4.
3 Follow potatoes recipe step 5 and roast recipe step 4.
4 Follow salad recipe step 13, potatoes recipe step 6, and serve with beef roast.

Monterey Beef Roast

1 Kg (2 lb) rib eye beef roast
125 g (4 oz) Dijon mustard, approximately
350 g (12 oz) coarse salt, approximately

Garnish the beef roast with watercress and a lemon twist, if desired, and serve the potatoes in their foil wrapping.

1. Using flexible-blade spatula or butter knife, spread meat evenly with a thick coat of mustard.
2. Pat on as much salt as will cling to the mustard.
3. When coals are covered with gray ash, gently place roast directly on top of them. Using tongs, give meat quarter turn every 10 minutes, always setting it down on top of fresh coals. Cook 25 to 30 minutes for rare, 30 to 35 minutes for medium rare, and 35 to 40 minutes for well done.
4. Transfer beef to platter and let rest 10 minutes.

Roast Potatoes with Herbed Butter

4 tablespoons unsalted butter
4 medium-size potatoes, suitable for roasting
1/4 teaspoon paprika
1/4 teaspoon dried leaf oregano
1/4 teaspoon dried basil, crumbled
1/4 teaspoon salt
Pinch of freshly ground pepper

1. Place butter in small bowl and allow to come to room temperature.
2. Scrub potatoes, rinse, and pat dry with paper towels. Cut potatoes crosswise into 5 mm (1/4 inch) slices without cutting through potato. Slices must stay attached.
3. Cut four 20 x 20 cm (8 x 8 inch) sheets of aluminium foil. Place each potato in centre of sheet, roll up edges, and crimp to seal. Place potatoes directly on hot coals and bake 40 minutes, turning several times during baking.
4. Add remaining ingredients to butter and stir to blend.
5. With tongs, transfer potatoes to platter. Open foil wrapping. With pastry brush, brush each potato with butter mixture, coating inside surfaces of each slice. Re-wrap loosely and return potatoes to coals. bake another 10 to 15 minutes, or until flesh yields easily when pressed.
6. With tongs, transfer potatoes to platter with beef, peel back foil, and serve.

Carrot and Broccoli Salad

Small bunch broccoli (about 500 g (1 lb))
2 large carrots
60 g (2 oz) jar pimentos
125 g (4 oz) jar capers
100 ml (3 fl oz) vegetable oil
2 tablespoons red wine vinegar
1/4 teaspoon salt
1/8 teaspoon pepper
Small head lettuce

1. Wash broccoli and cut into bite-size florets.
2. Scrape carrots, trim off ends, and cut on diagonal into 5 mm (1/4 inch) slices.
3. In medium-size saucepan, bring 2 1/2 cm (1 inch) of water to a boil over medium-high heat.
4. Add broccoli florets to boiling water, cover, and cook 1 minute, or until florets are crisp-tender.
5. With slotted spoon, transfer florets to colander, reserving cooking water, and refresh under cold running water 1 to 2 minutes. Keep water in pan boiling.
6. Add carrots to boiling water, cover, and cook 2 to 3 minutes, or until crisp-tender.
7. Add carrots to broccoli and refresh under cold running water 1 to 2 minutes.
8. Drain broccoli and carrots and turn into medium-size bowl.
9. In strainer, drain pimentos and chop enough to measure 2 tablespoons. Reserve remainder for other use.
10. In strainer, drain capers and, if salt-packed, rinse thoroughly under cold running water. Chop enough capers to measure 2 tablespoons
11. For dressing, combine oil, vinegar, pimentos, capers, salt, and pepper in small bowl and beat with fork. Pour dressing over vegetables and toss until vegetables are evenly coated. Cover with plastic wrap and refrigerate until ready to serve.
12. Wash lettuce and dry in salad spinner or pat dry with paper towels. Line serving platter with lettuce, cover with plastic wrap, and refrigerate until ready to serve.
13. Remove vegetables and platter from refrigerator. With wooden spoon, toss vegetables to recombine with dressing and spoon mixture onto lettuce-lined platter.

Roberta Rall

Menu 1
(*Right*)
Grilled Poussins
with Oriental Flavours
Stir-Fried Carrots with Snow Peas
Fresh Fruit in Cookie Cups

Home economist Roberta Rall keeps three questions in mind when she develops her recipes. First, does the recipe use time and ingredients economically? Menu 1 is an example of this practical approach. The marinade for the poussins is used as the cooking liquid for the stir-fried vegetables and, subsequently, it is served as a dunking sauce for the cooked poussins.

Second, are all the ingredients readily available? She suggests three choices of seafood for the entrée of Menu 2. Use either monkfish, shrimp, or catfish - depending on what is fresh in your marketplace. They are all firm-fleshed and therefore can be cooked on skewers without falling apart. If coriander, also known as Chinese parsley, is unavailable, use regular parsley instead. Substitutes will have a different flavour but will be just as delicious.

Third, can an inexperienced cook recreate the recipe? In Menu 3, she works with a basic dish that most home cooks know – hamburgers. To make these barbecued hamburgers special, she dresses them up with several variations: grated cheese, chopped avocado, sour cream, lettuce, and tomatoes or sautéed onions and mushrooms. Cooks can personalize the other components of the meal, too: For the raw vegetable platter and the fuit compote, select whatever seasonal produce suits your taste.

When you serve this barbecue, set one tray per guest, offering each a grilled poussin garnished with watercress and a portion of the stir-fried carrots, snow peas and water chestnuts. The baked cookie cups are filled with blueberries and raspberries.

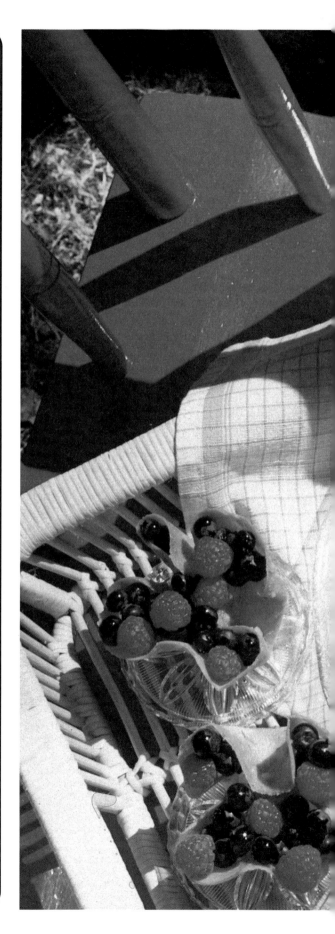

Menu 1

Grilled Poussins with Oriental Flavours
Stir-Fried Carrots with Snow Peas
Fresh Fruit in Cookie Cups

Marinated poussins, served hot from the barbecue grill, are the focal point of this meal. Bake the cookie cups first, then fill them with fruit just before serving.

Allow one bird per serving. Poussins have mild-flavoured white meat needing extra seasoning. For this recipe, they soak in a flavourful soy-based marinade that calls for Oriental sesame oil, an amber-coloured oil with an intense nutty flavour.

To stir-fry the carrots, snow peas, and water chestnuts, use a wok, the traditional Chinese pan used for quick cooking foods. Woks usually come with a lid, which allows you to steam, as you do with carrots in this recipe. Because they are firm, carrots require extra cooking before you add the water chestnuts and delicate snow peas. When all the vegetables are combined, stir them constantly with a Chinese metal wok spatula or long-handled spoons to keep them from scorching. If you have no wok, use a heavy-guage sauté pan.

The cookie cups are an adaption of the classic French *tuiles*– cookies shaped like the curved tiles on old French farmhouses. For this version, you push the baked, but still soft, cookies into custard cups, and the dough cools and hardens into an edible petal-shaped container for the fruit. If you wish, make the cookies ahead and store them in an airtight container. Because moisture from the fruit may cause the cookie bottoms to soften, fill the cookies just before serving.

What to drink

The flavours of this menu are somewhat spicy as well as slightly sweet, so your wine choice can accentuate either flavour. For a bit of sweetness, opt for a Riesling; for spiciness, choose a Gewürztraminer.

Start-to-Finish Steps

1 Start barbecue.
2 Follow poussins recipe steps 1 through 3.
3 While poussins are marinating, grind walnuts, grate orange peel, if using, and follow cookie cups recipe steps 1 through 6.
4 While cookies are baking, prepare fruit, if using, and refrigerate until ready to serve.
5 Follow poussins recipe step 4.
6 While poussins are grilling, follow carrots recipe steps 1 through 3.
7 If using watercress as garnish for poussins, wash and pat dry.
8 Five minutes before poussins are done, follow recipe step 5 and carrots recipe steps 4 and 5.
9 Follow poussins recipe step 6 and serve with carrots.
10 For dessert, follow cookie cups recipe step 7 and serve.

Grilled Poussins with Oriental Flavours

4 poussins (about 750 g (1¹/₂ lb) each)
4 cloves garlic
7¹/₂ cm (3 inch) piece fresh ginger
175 ml (6 fl oz) soy sauce
3 tablespoons peanut oil
1 tablespoon Oriental sesame oil
Watercress sprigs for garnish (optional)

1　With poultry or kitchen shears, remove backbones from poussins by cutting along each side of backbone until it is freed. Place poussins on work surface, skin side up, spread open, and, using mallet, pound breastbone so poussin will lie flat.

2　Peel and mince garlic and ginger.

3　For marinade, combine garlic, soy sauce, peanut oil, sesame oil, ginger, and 4 tablespoons water in large shallow baking dish. Add poussins and marinate, turning occasionally, at least 20 minutes.

4　Transfer poussins to grill, place cut side down, and cook, turning frequently and basting with marinade, about 30 minutes, or until tender and juices run clear when poussin is pierced with fork.

5　Reserve 3 tablespoons of marinade for carrots recipe and transfer remainder to small saucepan. Set on side of barbecue and bring to a simmer.

6　Transfer poussins to individual plates and garnish with watercress sprigs, if desired. Pour warmed marinade into individual bowls and serve as dipping sauce.

Stir-Fried Carrots with Snow Peas

3 carrots (about 125 g (4 oz))
60 g (2 oz) water chestnuts, drained
250 g (8 oz) snow peas
3 tablespoons reserved marinade from poussins

1　Peel carrots and cut on diagonal into 2¹/₂ mm (¹/₈ inch) slices.

2　Cut water chestnuts into 5 mm (¹/₄ inch) slices.

3　Top, tail, and string snow peas. Wash snow peas under cold running water and pat dry with paper towels.

4　In wok or large heavy-gauge skillet, heat reserved marinade over medium-high heat. Add carrots and cook, covered, 3 minutes.

5　Uncover pan, add chestnuts and snow peas, and stir fry about 3 minutes, or until vegetables are just crisp-tender. Remove pan from heat.

Fresh Fruit in Cookie Cups

4 tablespoons unsalted butter
1 egg
125 g (4 oz) confectioners' sugar
30 g (1 oz) ground walnuts
30 g (1 oz) plain flour
2 tablespoons milk
1 teaspoon grated orange peel (optional)
350 g (12 oz) summer berries (blueberries or raspberries), or 350 g (12 oz) cut-up fresh fruit of your choice (kiwis, grapes, orange sections, bananas, or papayas), or 4 scoops vanilla ice cream

1　Preheat oven to 190°C (375°F or Mark 5) and generously grease 2 baking sheets with 2 tablespoons butter.

2　Separate egg, placing white in medium-size bowl. Reserve yolk for another use.

3　Beat egg white with whisk or with electric beater on medium speed, until foamy, about 1 minute. Add sugar, walnuts, flour, milk, remaining butter, and orange peel, if using, and, with wooden spoon, stir to combine.

4　Place 2 cookies on each baking sheet, using 1¹/₂ to 2 tablespoons batter per cookie and spreading it into 15 cm (6 inch) circles.

5　Bake first batch of 4 cookies, turning sheets from back to front once, 8 to 10 minutes, or until edges of cookies are browned. Remove from oven and repeat with second batch.

6　As soon as first batch of cookies is done, remove each cookie with metal spatula and drape over a custard cup. Push cookie into cup with your fingers, moulding it to shape of cup. Top of cookie will flute naturally. Let stand 3 minutes. Remove cookies from custard cups and transfer to wire rack to cool. Repeat procedure with second batch of cookies.

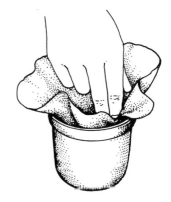

7　Just before serving, fill each cookie with fruit of your choice or ice cream.

Grilled Monkfish with Lime-Butter Baste
Marinated Vegetables
Bulgur with Carrots and Scallions

On a large serving platter, form a bed with the bulgur and top it with the skewered monkfish sprinkled with chopped coriander or parsley and scallions, if desired. Serve the marinated vegetables in a large bowl.

Because the fish grills quickly for this backyard barbecue, have the bulgur cooking and the vegetables marinating before putting the skewers on the grill.

Because of its texture, monkfish is especially good for skewer cooking, as are the optional firm-fleshed catfish and large shrimp.

Bulgur, sometimes mistakenly called cracked wheat, consists of whole wheat berries that are crushed, steam cooked, and then dried. It is a traditional Middle Eastern grain with a nutty taste and crunchy texture. Because bulgur has been processed, it tends to get mushy if you add too much liquid or cook it too long

What to drink
Iced tea would make a fine accompaniment to this meal. Alternatively, try a soft, dry white wine, either Italian Soave or a California Chenin Blanc.

Start-to-Finish Steps
1 Start barbecue.
2 Squeeze lemon juice for vegetables recipe and lime juice for vegetables and for monkfish recipes. Trim scallions, wash, and pat dry with paper towels. Cut 2 scallions into 5 mm (1/4 inch) thick rounds for vegetables recipe and chop 4 scallions for bulgur recipe.
3 Follow marinated vegetables recipe steps 1 and 2.
4 While vegetables are marinating, quarter limes, peel and devein shrimp, if using, and follow monkfish recipe steps 1 through 3.
5 Follow bulgur recipe steps 1 through 3.
6 Ten minutes before bulgur is done, follow monkfish recipe step 4, if cooking monkfish or catfish, or 8 minutes before it is done, if cooking shrimp.
7 While monkfish is grilling, wash lettuce and dry in salad spinner or pat dry with paper towels. Follow marinated vegetables recipe step 3.
8 Follow bulgur recipe step 4, monkfish recipe step 5, and serve with marinated vegetables.

Grilled Monkfish with Lime-Butter Baste

2 small cloves garlic
Small bunch coriander or parsley
125 g (4 oz) unsalted butter
2 tablespoons lime juice
1/2 teaspoon salt
2 limes, quartered
1 Kg (2 lb) monkfish or catfish, cut into 5 cm (2 inch) chunks (about 24 pieces), or 24 large shrimp

1 Peel and mince garlic. Wash and pat dry coriander or parsley. Finely chop enough coriander or parsley to measure 2 tablespoons plus 1 tablespoon for garnish, if using.
2 In small saucepan, combine garlic, butter, lime juice, and salt and heat over low heat, stirring occasionally with wooden spoon, until butter has melted. Off heat, stir in 2 tablespoons coriander or parsley.
3 On each of four long skewers, place 1 lime wedge, followed by 3 chunks of fish, another lime wedge, then 3 more chunks of fish, and finish the skewer with a lime wedge. Brush the fish with the melted lime butter.
4 Place skewers on grill set 10 cm (4 inches) from heat and cook, turning occasionally, 8 to 10 minutes (5 to 8 minutes for shrimp), or until fish flakes easily with tip of sharp knife (or until shrimp have firmed up and turned pinkish white).
5 Transfer skewers to platter with bulgur. Drizzle with remaining lime butter and sprinkle with 1 tablespoon chopped parsley or coriander.

Marinated Vegetables

2 small cloves garlic, peeled and crushed
150 ml (6 fl oz) vegetable oil
4 tablespoons fresh lemon juice
4 tablespoons fresh lime juice
2 tablespoons Dijon mustard
1 teaspoon sugar (optional)
2 scallions, cut into 5 mm (1/4 inch) rounds
1/2 tablespoon salt
Freshly ground black pepper
4 tomatoes, cored and thickly sliced
125 g (4 oz) mushrooms, thickly sliced
1 head leaf lettuce

1 In small bowl, combine garlic, oil, citrus juices, mustard, sugar, if using, scallions, salt, and pepper to taste and stir with fork until blended.

2 In shallow glass baking dish, arrange tomatoes and mushrooms in a single layer. Pour dressing over vegetables and marinate, turning vegetables occasionally, at least 30 minutes.
3 Just before serving, line salad bowl with lettuce. With slotted spoon, transfer tomatoes and mushrooms to lettuce-lined bowl. Spoon marinade over vegetables and sprinkle with a few grindings of black pepper, if desired.

Bulgur with Carrots and Scallions

2 medium-size carrots
2 tablespoons unsalted butter
125 g (4 oz) bulgur
4 scallions, chopped
250 ml (8 fl oz) chicken stock
1/4 teaspoon freshly ground black pepper
Salt

1 Peel carrots and, using large holes of grater, shred or cut carrots into julienne.
2 In medium-size heavy-gauge saucepan, melt butter over medium heat. Add carrot and sauté, stirring frequently, about 3 minutes. Add bulgur and scallions, and stir until evenly coated with butter. Add stock, 250 ml (8 fl oz) water, pepper, and salt to taste and stir to combine.
3 Bring mixture to a boil over medium-high heat. Reduce heat to a simmer, cover, and cook until bulgur is tender, 10 to 15 minutes.
4 Fluff bulgur with fork and turn onto serving platter.

Great Grilled Burgers
Raw Vegetables with Creamy Basil Dip
Fruit Layers with Vanilla Sauce

This barbecue is easy to organize: Have the raw vegetables with their dip and the fruit dessert ready and chilling before you grill the burgers. The main hamburger recipe calls for scallions, freshly ground pepper, and other seasonings. If you want to make the Mexican version, you will need a can of chilies and some chili powder. For the French variation, be sure you have some Burgundy wine and dried thyme on hand.

What to drink

Best bet with this straightforward menu would be ice-cold beer or ale. If you want wine, choose a simple red – a Beaujolais or a young, fruity Zinfandel.

Start-to-Finish Steps

1 Follow fruit layers recipe steps 1 through 3.
2 Start barbecue.
3 Follow vegetables recipe steps 1 through 3.
4 Follow burgers recipe steps 1 through 4 or make burger variation of your choice.
5 Follow burgers recipe step 5 and serve with vegetables and dip.
6 For dessert, serve fruit layers with vanilla sauce.

This casual barbecue consists of raw vegetables with a dip, hamburgers in one (or all) of three variations, and a fruit dessert.

Great Grilled Burgers

750 g (1 1/2 lb) minced beef
2 scallions, thinly sliced
4 tablespoons Worcestershire sauce
1 1/2 teaspoons salt
Freshly ground pepper
8 slices French or Italian bread
125 g (4 oz) cheddar, Jarlsberg, or Muenster,
  shredded, or 125 g (4 oz) blue cheese, crumbled

1 In medium-size bowl, combine minced beef with scallions, Worcestershire sauce, and salt.
2 Shape meat into 4 patties, each about 2 cm (3/4 inch) thick. Generously coat both sides of patties with pepper.
3 Place on grill and cook, turning once, to desired degree of doneness.
4 Five minutes before burgers are done, place bread on grill and toast about 2 minutes per side.
5 Transfer toasted bread to platter. With metal spatula, place 1 burger on each of 4 bread slices, top with cheese and remaining bread, and serve.

Burger Variations

Mexican Burgers: Combine minced beef with 1 teaspoon drained, chopped chilies, 1 1/2 teaspoons chili powder, and 1/2 teaspoon salt and proceed as for Great Grilled Burgers. Serve on toasted English muffins, topped with lettuce, tomato, avocado, and sour cream.

French Burgers: Combine minced beef with 4 tablespoons Burgundy, 1 teaspoon dried thyme, and 1/2 teaspoon salt and proceed as for Great Grilled Burgers. Serve on toasted slices of French or Italian bread, topped with 250 g (8 oz) chopped onions and 125 g (4 oz) sliced mushrooms that have been sautéed in 2 tablespoons unsalted butter.

Raw Vegetables with Creamy Basil Dip

125 g (4 oz) mushrooms
Large cucumber, cut into 1 cm (1/2 inch) julienne
2 red bell peppers, cut into 1 cm (1/2 inch) julienne
2 carrots, peeled and cut into 1 cm (1/2 inch) julienne
1 yellow squash, cut into 1 cm (1/2 inch) rounds
60 g (2 oz) fresh basil leaves, or 60 g (2 oz) parsley
  leaves plus 2 tablespoons dried basil, crushed
Small clove garlic, peeled and minced

250 ml (8 fl oz) sour cream
6 tablespoons mayonnaise
2 tablespoons grated Parmesan cheese
1 tablespoon cider vinegar
1/4 teaspoon freshly ground pepper
Salt

1 Wipe mushrooms with damp paper towels.
2 Arrange vegetables on platter, cover, and refrigerate.
3 In food processor or blender, combine fresh basil or parsley and dried basil, garlic, and remaining ingredients, and process until smooth. Scrape into small serving bowl, cover, and chill at least 45 minutes.

Fruit Layers with Vanilla Sauce

250 ml (8 fl oz) vanilla yogurt
2 tablespoons orange-flavored liqueur
1 cantaloupe, or 1/2 honeydew or other melon
3 kiwis, peeled and cut into rounds
3 nectarines, apples, or pears, sliced
250 g (8 oz) seedles red grapes, steamed

1 In small serving bowl, combine yogurt and liqueur, and stir until blended. Cover and chill at least 1 hour.
2 Halve melon, scoop out seeds, and discard. With melon baller, scoop out melon balls.
3 In medium-size glass serving bowl or carrying container, form individual layers of each fruit, adding them in the order listed. Cover and chill at least 45 minutes or until ready to serve.

Ron Davis

Menu 1
(*left*)
Duck, Chicken, and Veal Salad
Pasta with Three Cheeses
Asparagus with Garlic Dressing

Ron Davis has his own basic motto for successful cooking: 'Simplicity creates elegance.' He uses only the highest-quality products prepared to preserve their natural flavours. To do this, he avoids intricate seasonings and complex sauces that mask flavours. The barbecued river trout of Menu 2, with a fresh sautéed spinach and bread stuffing, for example, is enhanced by basting during cooking with the pan drippings from the sautéed spinach. Menu 1 features another straightforward approach. Strips of duck, chicken, and veal are first sautéed, then combined with raw vegetables and dressed with a lemon-, garlic-, and mustard-based mixture. He accompanies the meat with a chilled pasta dish – spirals and shells dressed with Roquefort, Parmesan, and Romano cheeses.

Ron Davis describes himself as an American cook who draws upon all the available influences, and Menu 3 is an example of how he structures an American meal: the spareribs are Southwestern, and the scallop seviche, Mexican.

Organize this elegant picnic in three wicker baskets: in one, put the duck, chicken, and veal salad; in the second, the pasta salad with cheese dressing; and in the third, the bundled asparagus spears with garlic dressing.

Duck, Chicken, and Veal Salad
Pasta with Three Cheeses
Asparagus with Garlic Dressing

This picnic features two main-dish salads. Chill the two salad dressings and the garlic dip for the asparagus spears while you prepare the rest of the meal. Combine the pasta and the meat salads with their respective dressings, then pack the meat salad and the asparagus dip in an ice chest for transporting to the picnic. You must do this to keep the egg-based dressings chilled.

What to drink
For a red wine, try a young Zinfandel or Chianti; for white, a California Sauvignon or an Italian Chardonnay.

Start-to-Finish Steps
1   Follow pasta recipe step 1.
2   While water is coming to a boil, prepare herbs and juice lemon. Grate Parmesan and Romano, and combine in small bowl.
3   Follow pasta recipe steps 2 through 8.
4   Follow salad recipe steps 1 through 5.
5   Follow asparagus recipe steps 1 through 5.
6   Follow salad recipe steps 6 and 7.
7   Follow pasta recipe step 9, salad recipe step 8, and pack with asparagus and dressing.
8   Before serving, toss salads and stir dressing.

Duck, Chicken, and Veal Salad

1 breast of duck, boned and skinned
2 whole chicken breasts, boned and skinned
500 g (1 lb) veal scaloppine, pounded to 2½ mm (⅛ inch) thickness
60 g (2 oz) plain flour
4 tablespoons olive oil
1 tablespoon unsalted butter
4 tablespoons dry white wine or dry vermouth
Medium-size red bell pepper
3 stalks celery
Small onion
2 tablespoons chopped parsley
1 tablespoon chopped dill
Salt and freshly ground white pepper
Salad dressing (see following recipe)

1   Cut duck, chicken, and veal into strips.
2   Dredge veal lightly with flour.
3   In large sauté pan, heat 2 tablespoons olive oil over medium heat. Add veal strips and sauté 3 to 4 minutes.
4   Drain well in colander and then transfer to large bowl.
5   In same sauté pan, heat butter and remaining olive oil over medium heat. Add poultry and sauté 4 to 5 minutes. Just before removing from heat, add wine or vermouth and toss strips until coated. Drain and transfer to bowl with veal.
6   Core, seed, and halve red pepper. Cut pepper and celery into 5 mm (¼ inch) dice. Peel and dice onion.
7   Add vegetables to veal and poultry strips and, with wooden spoon, toss gently to combine. Add parsley, dill, salt, and white pepper to taste, and toss.
8   Pour dressing over salad and toss to coat. Turn into large carrying container with lid.

Salad Dressing

2 egg yolks
Juice of ½ lemon
2 tablespoons red wine vinegar
¼ teaspoon minced garlic, crushed
1 small shallot, minced
½ teaspoon Dijon mustard
Pinch of Cayenne pepper
Pinch of salt
125 ml (4 fl oz) olive oil
150 ml (5 fl oz) vegetable oil

1   In medium-size bowl, combine egg yolks, lemon juice, vinegar, garlic, shallot, mustard, Cayenne, and salt. With electric mixer at low speed or with whisk, beat briefly.
2   In measuring cup, combine olive oil and vegetable oil.
3   Beating constantly at low speed, slowly drizzle oil into yolk mixture. Increase speed to medium and beat steadily until dressing is thick and smooth.
4   Cover and refrigerate until ready to pack.

Pasta with Three Cheeses

Salt
5 large mushrooms
250 g (8 oz) small pasta shells
250 g (8 oz) small pasta spirals
$^1/_2$ teaspoon minced garlic, crushed
3 tablespoons chopped basil
4 tablespoons olive oil
1 tablespoon chopped parsley
Juice of $^1/_2$ lemon
1 teaspoon red wine vinegar
125 g (4 oz) broccoli florets (optional)
12 cherry tomatoes (optional)
125 g (4 oz) pitted black olives (optional)
3 tablespoons unsalted butter
$^1/_4$ teaspoon freshly ground black pepper
125 g (4 oz) Roquefort cheese, crumbled
60 g (2 oz) freshly grated Parmesan cheese
60 g (2 oz) freshly grated Romano cheese

1   In large saucepan or stockpot, bring 4 teaspoons salt and 6 ltrs (8 pts) cold water to a boil.
2   Cut mushrooms into 5 mm ($^1/_4$ inch) slices.
3   Cook pasta according to package directions, adding shells 4 minutes after adding spirals.
4   While pasta is cooking, combine garlic, basil, oil, parsley, lemon juice, and vinegar in bowl of processor or blender and process about 1 minute, or until smooth. Cover bowl and refrigerate until ready to pack picnic.
5   If using broccoli, bring 1$^1/_4$ ltrs (2 pts) water and 1 teaspoon salt to a boil in a small saucepan. Add florets and blanch 1 minute. Turn into colander, refresh under cold running water, and drain. Halve tomatoes, if using. In large bowl, combine broccoli, tomatoes, and olives, if using.
6   In colander, drain pasta and rinse under cold running water. Refill pan with cold water and return pasta to pan.
7   In medium-size sauté pan, melt butter over medium heat. Add mushrooms and pepper, and sauté 3 to 4 minutes.
8   Drain cooled pasta thoroughly and add to vegetables.
9   Add cheeses to pasta mixture and toss to combine. Add dressing and toss gently until evenly coated. Turn into large carrying container with lid.

Asparagus with Garlic Dressing

Salt
750 g (1$^1/_2$ lb) asparagus spears of uniform size
4 tablespoons mayonnaise
150 ml (5 fl oz) sour cream
$^1/_2$ teaspoon minced garlic
1 tablespoon chopped parsley
$^1/_4$ teaspoon freshly ground white pepper
Pinch of Cayenne pepper

1   Break off tough bottom stems of asparagus spears. Wash asparagus and gently pat dry with paper towels.
2   In large skillet, bring 1 teaspoon salt and 5 cm (2 inches) of water to a rolling boil.
3   While water is heating, combine remaining ingredients and salt to taste in small bowl, and stir until blended. Transfer dressing to jar with lid or other carrying container and refrigerate until ready to pack picnic.
4   Add asparagus to boiling water and cook, uncovered, just until bright green and crisp-tender, 1 to 2 minutes.
5   In colander, drain asparagus and leave under cold running water until completely cool, about 3 minutes. Drain and pat dry. Wrap securely in plastic wrap.

<table>
<tr><td>

</td><td>

Grilled River Trout with Spinach, Bread, and Vegetable Stuffing
Tomato, Onion, and Watercress Salad
Leeks with Roasted Pepper and Bucheron Cheese

</td></tr>
</table>

A whole river trout looks dramatic in any setting. Here it is garnished with sliced tomatoes, lemons, and watercress sprigs. Leeks with red peppers and Bûcheron and the salad are served in separate containers.

Since you will be cooking the fish last for this barbecue, dress the leeks and the salad just before the fish is ready to be served.

Stuffed with a spinach filling, then tied up for barbecuing, the trout cooks over the hot coals in a hinged wire basket that closes tightly around the fish and prevents it from breaking apart and falling into the fire. You can easily turn the long-handled basket to control the speed at which the fish cooks. If you have no basket, you can wrap the fish in foil and cook it on the grill, but the skin will not get crisp.

What to drink
These sharp, clear flavours need a firm, dry white wine: A California Chardonnay, an Alsation sylvaner, or a white Graves are all good choices.

Start-to-Finish Steps
1 Start barbecue.
2 Peel, mince, and crush garlic for all recipes. Peel, mince, and crush shallot for leeks recipe. Wash, pat dry, and chop parsley, dill, and fresh basil, if using, for trout. Juice lemons for all recipes. Follow trout recipe steps 1 through 3.
3 While vegetable mixture is cooking, follow leeks recipe steps 1 and 2.
4 Follow trout recipe step 4.
5 While spinach is cooking, follow salad recipe step 1.
6 Follow trout recipe step 5 and leeks recipe step 3.
7 While leeks are poaching, follow salad recipe steps 2 and 3.
8 Follow leeks recipe steps 4 through 7 and salad recipe steps 4 through 7.
9 Follow trout recipe steps 6 through 10.
10 Follow salad recipe step 8 and leeks recipe step 8.
11 When barbecue is ready, follow trout recipe step 11.
12 Five minutes before fish is done, follow salad recipe step 9 and leeks recipe step 9.
13 Follow trout recipe steps 12 and 13, and serve with salad and leeks.

26

Grilled River Trout with Spinach, Bread, and Vegetable Stuffing

350 g (12 oz) spinach
Medium-size red bell pepper
Medium-size yellow onion
250 g (8 oz) tomatoes, plus one for garnish (optional)
125 g (4 oz) fresh cultivated mushrooms
2 tablespoons clarified butter
3/4 teaspoon minced garlic
Juice of 1 medium-size lemon
1 teaspoon chopped fresh parsley
1 teaspoon chopped fresh dill
1 1/2 teaspoons chopped basil, or 1/2 teaspoon dried
125 ml (4 fl oz) dry white wine
Watercress sprigs for garnish (optional)
1 lemon for garnish (optional)
5 slices white or whole-wheat bread (about 125 g (4 oz))
1 egg
Salt and freshly ground pepper
1 1/2 Kg (3 lb) river trout, dressed and boned

1 In colander, wash spinach thoroughly under cold running water. Dry in salad spinner or pat dry with paper towels. Chop coarsely into 2 1/2 cm (1 inch) strips.

2 Wash red pepper and pat dry with paper towels. Core, seed, and halve pepper. Cut into 1/2–1 cm (1/4-1/2 inch) dice. Peel onion and and dice. Wash tomatoes and pat dry with paper towels. Slice one for garnish, if using. Core, halve, seed and dice remaining tomatoes. Wipe mushrooms with damp paper towels and cut into 5 mm (1/4 inch) slices.

3 In large sauté pan, heat clarified butter over medium high heat. Add red pepper, tomatoes, mushrooms, garlic, lemon juice, parsley, dill, and basil. Sauté mixture, stirring frequently with wooden spoon, about 5 minutes.

4 Add spinach and wine, and stir to combine. Cook spinach, stirring frequently, until wilted but still bright green, about 5 minutes.

5 Set strainer over medium-size bowl. Turn spinach mixture into strainer and drain thoroughly. Transfer vegetable liquid to jar with lid or other carrying container for transport.

6 Prepare garnishes, if using: Wash watercress and dry in salad spinner or pat dry with paper towels; wash tomato, pat dry, and cut crosswise into slices; cut lemon into thin slices. Wrap in plastic for transport.

7 With your fingers, tear bread into small pieces and place them in medium-size mixing bowl. Add drained vegetable mixture and toss to combine.

8 In small bowl, beat egg with fork. Add egg to stuffing mixture and stir until blended. Add salt and pepper to taste. If mixture seems dry, add a little of the reserved vegetable liquid and stir until incorporated. Mixture should be just barely wet enough to hold together.

9 Spread trout open and fill cavity with stuffing. Do not overfill; stuffing will expand during cooking.

10 Use cord to tie fish securely but not too tightly. Strips of foil may be used instead of cord. Wrap fish in aluminium foil for transport.

11 Unwrap fish and place in grilling basket. Set basket on hot grill 10 cm (4 inches) from heat and cook about 25 minutes, or until fish is flaky but still moist, reversing basket several times to grill both sides of fish evenly. Through basket, baste frequently with vegetable liquids.

12 Remove fish from grill. Open basket, lay platter over side of basket that contains fish, and invert so that fish drops onto platter. Cut strings tying fish, remove, and discard.

13 Serve the fish garnished with watercress sprigs, tomato, and lemon slices, if desired.

Tomato, Onion, and Watercress Salad

2 bunches fresh watercress
Small red onion
1 teaspoon sesame seeds
Medium-size navel orange
500 g (1 lb) tomatoes
Salt and freshly ground pepper
2 tablespoons red wine vinegar
1 teaspoon tamari, or ¹/₂ teaspoon soy sauce
Juice of ¹/₂ medium-size lemon
4 tablespoons blended oil (any oil but olive)

1   Soak greens in bowl of cold water for 5 minutes.
2   Dry greens in salad spinner or pat dry with paper towels. Remove stems and discard.
3   Peel onion and cut into thin slices.
4   In small heavy-gauge skillet, toast sesame seeds over medium heat, shaking skillet frequently, until they turn golden brown and release their fragrance, about 3 to 4 minutes.
5   Trim peel and white pith from orange. Then, over salad bowl, holding orange in one hand and knife in other, free segments by cutting toward centre on each side of membranes, letting segments fall into bowl.
6   Wash tomatoes and pat dry with paper towels. Core tomatoes and, with chef's knife, chop coarsely into 2¹/₂ cm (1 inch) chunks. Place chunks in salad bowl.
7   Add sliced onion to tomatoes and mix well. Add watercress, orange sections, sesame seeds, and salt and pepper to taste, and toss to combine. Cover with plastic wrap and refrigerate until ready to leave.

8   For dressing, combine vinegar, tamari or soy, lemon juice, and oil in small jar with lid or other carrying container.
9   Just before serving, shake or stir dressing to recombine. Pour over salad and toss gently.

Leeks with Roasted Pepper and Bûcheron Cheese

Salt
4 small leeks
250 g (8 oz) roasted red peppers
Small head red or green leaf lettuce
30 g (1 oz) crumbled Bûcheron cheese or any sharp chèvre or feta cheese
1 shallot, minced
¹/₂ teaspoon minced garlic
4 teaspoons Dijon mustard
2 tablespoons red wine vinegar
Juice of ¹/₂ medium-size lemon
¹/₄ teaspoon freshly ground black pepper
125 ml (4 fl oz) blended oil (any oil but olive)

1   In medium-size skillet, bring enough water to cover leeks plus 1 teaspoon salt per 1 ltr (2 pts) water to the boil.
2   With chef's knife, trim leeks, leaving approximately 5 cm (2 inches) of green. Split leeks lengthwise, spread leaves, and wash thoroughly in cold water.
3   Add leeks to boiling water, reduce heat to a simmer, cover, and cook until leeks are tender, 6 to 7 minutes.
4   With slotted spoon, transfer leeks to colander and refresh under cold running water.
5   In strainer, rinse roasted peppers under cold running water. Chop enough pepper to measure 125 g (4 oz). Set aside.
6   Remove outer leaves from lettuce, discarding any that are badly bruised and reserving inside leaves for another use. Wash leaves under cold running water and dry in salad spinner or pat dry with paper towels.
7   On platter, arrange a bed of lettuce leaves. Top with leeks and sprinkle with crumbled Bûcheron and chopped pepper. Cover with plastic wrap and refrigerate.
8   In small bowl, combine shallot, garlic, mustard, vinegar, lemon juice, and pepper. Beating constantly with whisk, add oil in a slow, steady stream, and beat until oil is totally incorporated. Transfer mixture to small jar with lid or other carrying container.
9   Just before serving, shake or stir dressing to recombine and pour over salad.

Apple Crumble Pie

125 g (4 oz) sifted plain flour 100 g (3 oz) sifted plain
   or whole-wheat flour
$^3/_4$ teaspoon salt
350 g (12 oz) chilled unsalted butter
1 lemon
1 Kg (2 lb) tart eating apples
125 g (5 oz) firmly packed dark brown sugar
$^1/_2$ teaspoon freshly grated nutmeg
$^1/_2$ teaspoon cinnamon
250 ml (8 fl oz) heavy cream (optional)

1   Preheat oven to 180°C (350°F or Mark 4).
2   Sift together 125 g (4 oz) cup flour and $^1/_2$
    teaspoon salt. Set aside.
3   Line counter or cutting board with several sheets
    of wax paper. With chef's knife, cut $^1/_3$ of butter
    into 32 little cubes. Separate cubes.
4   In medium-size bowl, combine the $^1/_3$ of butter
    with flour-salt mixture and refrigerate remaining.
5   With pastry blender or two knives, cut butter into
    flour until mixture resembles coarse meal. Add 2
    to 3 tablespoons cold water or just enough to make
    the mixture cohere without becoming sticky. Form
    mixture into ball.
6   Lightly flour rolling surface and rolling pin. Roll
    dough out into circle large enough to fit 22$^1/_2$ cm
    (9 inch) pie plate. Gently fold dough in half and
    then into quarters. Carefully transfer dough to pie
    plate and unfold, lining plate.
7   Juice lemon and set aside.
8   Peel, halve, and core apples. With chef's knife, cut
    each half into 1 cm ($^1/_2$ inch) thick crescents and
    place in large mixing bowl. Add reserved lemon
    juice and toss until coated.
9   Arrange apple crescents in crust-lined pie plate.
10 Wipe out bowl with paper towels and into it sift
    remaining flour, brown sugar, and $^1/_4$ teaspoon
    salt. Remove remaining butter from refrigerator
    and add to bowl. Using pastry blender or 2 knives,
    cut butter into mixture until it is crumbly and well-
    combined.
11 Sprinkle apples with nutmeg and cinnamon, and
    then with crumb mixture. Do not combine.
12 Bake pie 45 minutes.
13 Serve hot or cold with pouring cream or whipped
    cream, if desired. If serving whipped cream, chill
    bowl and beaters for ten minutes. Pour cream into
    bowl and beat at slow and then medium speed
    until a spoonful is thick enough just to hold a
    shape, 3 to 4 minutes.

Scallop Seviche
Sweet-and-Spicy Barbecued Spareribs
Honey-Mustard Coleslaw

Prepare the coleslaw and scallop seviche completely ahead of time. To ready the spareribs for the barbecue, precook them either the night before the barbecue or 1 hour ahead. Not only does this shorten barbecuing time, it also prevents the meat from toughening on the hot grill.

What to drink

Ice-cold beer or ale is a classic accompaniment to spareribs. You might like to try a dark English ale here. For wine, choose a good Gewürztraminer from Alsace or California, lightly chilled.

Start-to-Finish Steps

The night before or 1 hour ahead: In large covered stockpot , bring 6 ltrs (8 pts) water to a boil. Add ribs to boiling water, cover, and cook 25 minutes. Drain and pat dry. Refrigerate overnight or proceed with recipe.

Thirty minutes ahead: Start barbecue.

1. Wash, pat dry, and chop parsley for all recipes. Wash, pat dry, and chop coriander for seviche. Juice lemons for all recipes. Juice limes for seviche. If using sea scallops, quarter them and follow seviche recipe steps 1 through 4.
2. Follow ribs recipe steps 1 through 3.
3. While barbecue sauce is simmering, follow coleslaw recipe steps 1 through 7.
4. Follow ribs recipe steps 4 through 6.
5. Ten minutes before ribs are done, while continuing to baste and turn ribs, follow seviche recipe step 5 and serve.
6. Follow ribs recipe step 7 and serve with coleslaw.

The colourful coleslaw, served in a large salad bowl, is a prominent part of this barbecue. Offer the scallop and avocado seviche as an appetizer or serve it as an accompaniment to the spareribs.

Scallop Seviche

500 g (1 lb) scallops
150 ml (5 fl oz) lime juice
15 g (¹/₂ oz) chopped parsley
30 g (1 oz) chopped coriander
Medium-size avocado
2 tablespoons lemon juice
Small bunch spinach

1   In medium-size bowl, combine scallops and lime juice, parsley and coriander, and toss.
2   Peel avocado. Cut in half lengthwise, remove pit and dice into pieces approximately the same size as the scallops. In small bowl, combine avocado with lemon juice and toss gently. Let stand 5 minutes.
3   Place spinach in colander, wash thoroughly, and dry in salad spinner. Discard stems. Wrap in paper towels and refrigerate.
4   With a slotted spoon, transfer avocado to bowl with scallops and toss gently. Refrigerate, covered, about 1¹/₂ hrs.
5   Line bowl with spinach leaves. Transfer seviche to bowl with a slotted spoon. Serve.

Sweet-and-Spicy Barbecued Spareribs

2 racks spare ribs (about 3 Kg (6 lbs) total weight)
3 small cloves garlic
Medium-size onion
1.5 Kg (3 lbs) Italian plum tomatoes
125 g (4 oz) unsalted butter
1/4 teaspoon ground cumin
1/2 teaspoon chili powder
1 tablespoon chopped parsley
1/2 teaspoon Cayenne pepper
3/4 teaspoon freshly ground black pepper
1 tablespoon red wine vinegar
Juice of 1/2 lemon
175 g (6 oz) tomato paste
4 tablespoons liquid brown sugar or dark cane syrup,
    or 3 tablespoons brown sugar plus 1/2 teaspoon
    maple syrup
100 mls (3 fl oz) dry red wine

1   Place grill 20 cm (8 inches) from coals and on it arrange precooked ribs in single layer. Barbecue ribs, turning often, for 20 minutes, or until ribs lose their raw look.
2   Peel and chop garlic. Peel and chop onion. Wash, dry, core, and quarter tomatoes.

3   In large saucepan, combine garlic, onion, tomatoes, butter, cumin, chili powder, parsley, Cayenne, black pepper, vinegar, and lemon juice. Bring to a simmer over low heat and, stirring occasionally with wooden spoon, simmer, covered, about 15 minutes.
4   Uncover pan and add tomato paste, liquid brown sugar or dark cane syrup (or brown sugar and maple syrup), and wine. Return to a simmer and cook, stirring, an additional 5 minutes, or until thick and smooth. Remove pan from heat.
5   Pour sauce into blender, a little at a time, and blend until smooth, about 45 seconds. Transfer sauce to large mixing bowl.
6   Baste ribs with barbecue sauce, turning frequently, until crusty with sauce and a dark brick-red colour, another 25 minutes.
7   Transfer ribs to platter and serve.

Honey-Mustard Coleslaw

250 g (8 oz) white cabbage
250 g (8 oz) red cabbage
Small courgette
Small carrot
1 shallot
12 small sweet gherkins
Juice of 1 lemon
1 tablespoon white wine vinegar
1 tablespoon chopped dill
1 tablespoon chopped parsley
4 tablespoons prepared honey-mustard (or equal parts
    Dijon mustard and honey)
150 g (5 oz) good-quality commercial mayonnaise
Salt and freshly ground pepper

1   Peel off tough outer leaves of cabbages and discard.
2   In food processor or large holes of grater, thinly shred cabbages. Transfer to large mixing bowl and, with your hands, toss to mix colours. Wash courgette and carrot and pat dry with paper towels.
3   Peel carrot. Shred courgette and carrot in food processor or on large holes of grater.
4   Peel and mince shallot. Cut sweet gherkins into 1/2–1 cm (1/4-1/2 inch) slices.
5   Add vegetables, shallot, gherkins, lemon juice, vinegar, dill, and parsley to bowl with cabbages and, with your hands, toss to combine.
6   If making your own honey-mustard, combine 2 tablespoons Dijon mustard and 2 tablespoons honey in small bowl. Spoon mustard over slaw, add mayonnaise, and toss with salad server until blended. Add salt and pepper to taste and toss again.
7   Cover and chill thoroughly before serving.

Added touch

The cook advises you not to bake this rich dark bread if the weather is rainy or very humid because the dough will not rise properly.

Black Bread

175 g (6 oz) fine bread crumbs
4 tablespoons blackstrap molasses
4 teaspoons instant coffee
1 teaspoon sugar
½ teaspoon ground ginger
2 sachets active dry yeast
4 tablespoons unsalted butter
350 g (12 oz) rye flour
2 teaspoons salt
225 g (7 oz) plain flour
1 egg

1 Preheat oven to 180°C (350°F or Mark 4).
2 Spread bread crumbs in baking pan and toast in oven, shaking pan occasionally, until golden brown, 7 to 10 minutes.
3 Turn off oven, remove crumbs, and let cool.
4 In large mixing bowl, combine 2 cups hot water, molasses, and 3 teaspoons instant coffee, and stir until dissolved. Add cooled bread crumbs and stir until blended.
5 In small bowl, combine 125 ml (4 fl oz) lukewarm water, sugar, ginger, and yeast, and stir with fork until blended. Let stand about 15 minutes, or until mixture starts to foam.
6 In small saucepan, melt butter over low heat.
7 To form dough, add yeast mixture to molasses mixture and stir to combine. Slowly add rye flour, stirring with wooden spoon until completely incorporated. Add melted butter and salt, and stir until blended.
8 Turn 175 g (6 oz) plain flour out onto large board. Place rye dough in centre of flour and cover with inverted bowl. Let dough rest 15 minutes.
9 Uncover dough. Incorporating the plain flour as you work, knead dough about 10 minutes, or until firm and no longer sticky.
10 Lightly butter large mixing bowl. Turn dough into bowl, cover with clean towel, and allow to rise in draught-free area until double in bulk, 1½ to 2 hours.
11 Lightly flour board. Turn dough out onto board and knead 5 minutes.
12 Butter baking pan and sprinkle with flour.
13 Shape dough into round or oblong loaf. Using your hands or 2 metal spatulas, carefully lift loaf onto baking sheet. Cover with towel and allow to rise until double in bulk, 30 to 60 minutes.
14 Preheat oven to 200°C (400°F or Mark 6).
15 Combine 1 teaspoon instant coffee with 3 tablespoons hot water in small bowl or cup and stir to dissolve. Set aside to cool.
16 In small bowl, beat egg lightly with fork. Add cooled instant-coffee mixture and beat lightly until combined.
17 With pastry brush, coat bread with coffee-egg glaze.
18 Place bread in oven and bake 40 to 45 minutes, or until bread has crisp crust and has a hollow sound when tapped with your fist.
19 Remove bread from oven and place on rack to cool. If packing up for picnic, cool at least 1 hour before wrapping in foil.

33

Victoria Wise

Menu 1
(*Right*)
Salmon Barbecued with Fennel,
Lemon, and Onion
Grilled Corn
Cucumbers and Radishes with Watercress

Victoria Wise spent her childhood in Japan and has
lived in the south of France, where she apprenticed in
a *charcuterie* – the French version of a delicatessen.
This diverse background influences her cooking and
menu planning. She uses classic French cooking
tequniques, yet she likes unorthodox combinations of
flavours and ingredients. Today she works in California,
where cooks have abundant seasonal produce and
fresh aromatic herbs year round.

Californians love to barbecue, says Victoria Wise,
and barbecuing is one of her specialities. Her salmon
recipe was inspired by the aromatic herb fennel.
Victoria Wise says that the herb grows wild throughout
California, but, if picking your own, be careful, as
many poisonous plants resemble it.

Menu 2 shows southern European influences. A
Mediterranean summer meal, it features grilled
marinated rabbit accompanied by a Greek tomato
salad and an Italian-style dish of grilled yellow and
green peppers with olive oil and garlic.

Her third menu is Provençal: artichokes cooked
with lemon, oregano, and garlic, and pork loin roasted
with garlic and sage. Both are served with tapénade,
a sauce containing capers whose name comes from
the Provencal word for caper – *tapéno*.

*A grilled salmon fillet, garnished with thin slices of lemon
and a sprig of feathery fennel and served on a plank, is an
impressive main course for this barbecue. With the grilled
corn, offer guests an empty bowl for discarding the husks
and silk. serve the sald in individual bowls.*

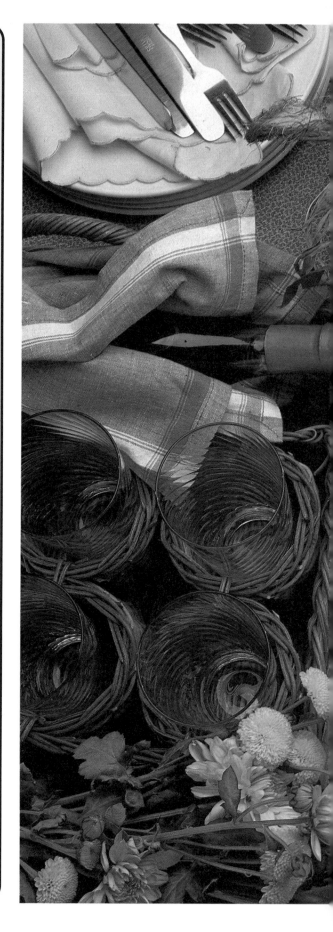

Salmon Barbecued with Fennel, Lemon, and Onion
Grilled Corn
Cucumbers and Radishes with Watercress

For this barbecue, first make the salad. Then, refrigerate the salad or store it in a chilled container while grilling the salmon and the corn.

The rich taste of the salmon is enhanced here by barbecuing. For further flavouring, it is grilled directly on top of stalks of fennel, a herb that is not widely available outside of California. Alternatively, buy the feathery top stalks of the vegetable fennel, or, if it, too, is unavailable, sprinkle fennel seeds on top of the fish or over the hot coals. You can also lay stalks of fresh dill under the grilling salmon, or sprinkle a combination of fennel seeds and dill on the salmon as it cooks.

What to drink

The best beverages for this menu are beer or iced tea. If you really prefer wine, try a dry and spicy California or Alsatian Gewürztraminer.

Start-to-Finish Steps

1 Start barbecue, using masquite, if available.
2 Follow salad recipe steps 1 through 5.
3 Follow salmon recipe steps 1 through 5.
4 When coals are covered with white ash, place grill rack 10 cm (4 inches) from them and heat 2 to 3 minutes.
5 Follow corn recipe step 1 and salmon recipe step 6.
6 Follow salmon recipe step 7, corn recipe step 2, salad recipe step 6, and serve.

Salmon Barbecued with Fennel, Lemon, and Onion

1.25 Kg (2½ lb) salmon fillet, about 4 cm (1¾ inches) thick at thickest point
3 tablespoons olive oil
Medium-size onion
3 lemons
6 fresh fennel stalks with greens (not bulbs) plus greens for garnish (optional), or small bunch fresh dill, preferably long-stemmed, or 2 teaspoons dried dill plus ½ teaspoon fennel seeds.
Salt and freshly ground black pepper

1 Wipe salmon with damp paper towels.
2 Spoon oil over salmon and, with your fingers, coat both sides evenly.

3 Peel onion and slice thinly.
4 Cut lemons into 2½–5 mm (⅛-¼ inch) slices. Wash fresh dill, if using, and pat dry.
5 Top salmon with single layer of onion slices and slices of 1 lemon. If using dried dill and fennel seeds, scatter over onion and lemon.
6 Lay fennel stalks or fresh dill on top of hot grill and place salmon on top of them. Cover barbecue with hood and cook with vent open 20 to 30 minutes.
7 Using 2 metal spatulas, transfer salmon to cutting board or platter, sprinkle with salt and pepper to taste, and garnish with lemon slices and fennel greens, if desired.

Grilled Corn

6 to 8 ears tender young corn, unhusked
125 g (4 oz) unsalted butter, approximately
Salt and freshly ground black pepper

1 Place unhusked corn on grill. Cover barbecue and cook corn with vent open, 30 minutes, turning occasionally.
2 Serve corn in husks, accompanied by butter, salt, and freshly ground black pepper.

Cucumbers and Radishes with Watercress

2 medium-size cucumbers (about 500 g (1 lb) total weight)
1 bunch red radishes
6 sprigs parsley
Large bunch watercress
2 lemons
1 lime
¼ teaspoon salt
3 tablespoons olive oil

1 Wash cucumbers thoroughly and pat dry with paper towels. With vegetable peeler, remove alternate lengths of peel to create a striped effect. Halve cucumbers lengthwise and, if necessary, remove seeds with melon baller or teaspoon.

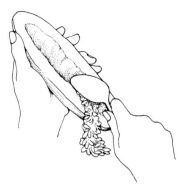

Place cucumbers cut side down and, with chef's knife, cut into 1 cm (1/2 inch) slices. Transfer slices to medium-size bowl.

2 Trim radishes, wash, and pat dry with paper towels. With paring knife, cut into 1 cm (1/2 inch) rounds. Add radishes to bowl.

3 Keeping parsley and watercress separate, remove stems, wash, and pat dry with paper towels. With chef's knife, mince parsley and add to bowl. Reserve watercress.

4 Juice lemons and lime. In small bowl, combine juices, salt, and olive oil, and stir with fork until blended.

5 Line small canning jars or small bowls with reserved watercress.

6 Pour dressing over salad and toss. Spoon salad into watercress-lined jars or bowls.

Added touch

This berry tart can be flavoured with kirschwasser, a cherry-flavoured brandy, or with another *eau de vie* (clear fruit brandy) such as Calvados, Poire Williams, or Mirabelle. Serve plain or with whipped cream or créme fraîche.

Berry Tart

7 tablespoons unsalted butter
125 g (4 oz) plus 1 tablespoon sifted flour
2 tablespoons sugar
500 g (1 lb) fresh berries
1 tablespoon lemon juice
175 g (6 oz) red currant jelly
1 1/2 tablespoons Kirschwasser, other *eau de vie*, or Port

1 Cut butter into 1-tablespoon pieces and allow to come to room temperature.

2 Sift flour and sugar together into medium-size bowl.

3 Add butter and, with your fingers, work into dry ingredients until mixture resembles coarse meal. Add 1 tablespoon cold water and work flour-butter mixture until you can gather it all into a ball. If necessary, add a few extra drops of cold water very sparingly.

4 Wrap dough in plastic wrap and flatten slightly with your palm. Refrigerate dough at least 1 hour or overnight.

5 Remove dough from refrigerator and let stand at room temperature until malleable, about 1 hour. Or, soften partially by beating dough, still wrapped in plastic, with rolling pin, turning dough as you beat it. Then, leave dough to warm and soften.

6 When dough is malleable, line 22 1/2 cm (9 inch) tart mould with removable bottom by pressing dough evenly against bottom and sides. Refrigerate at least 30 minutes.

7 Preheat oven to 200°C (400°F or Mark 6).

8 Prick bottom of tart 5 or 6 times with fork. Place mould in oven and bake until crust is golden brown and cooked through, about 20 minutes. If bottom begins to puff during baking, prick it with fork a few more times.

9 Remove mould from oven and set on rack to cool.

10 In colander, rinse berries, hull if necessary, and gently dry with paper towels.

11 For glaze, combine lemon juice, red currant jelly, and kirschwasser, *eau de vie*, or Port in small saucepan. Stirring constantly with whisk, bring to a boil over medium heat. Lower heat to a simmer and reduce glaze until it registers 100°C (200°F) on candy thermometer, about 3 minutes. Remove pan from heat.

12 With pastry brush, lightly paint bottom and sides of shell with glaze. Reserve remaining glaze.

13 Starting at centre and working outward, arrange berries in tart shell. If using strawberries, place them hulled side down. Using pastry brush, spread remaining glaze evenly over berries.

14 Serve at room temperature or refrigerate for up to 3 hours.

15 To serve, support bottom of tart ring with your hand and pushing upward, gently separate tart from sides of ring. Place tart with ring bottom on serving plate.

Grilled Rabbit
Grilled Yellow and Green Bell Peppers
Mediterranean Tomato Salad

Serve the rabbit and the green and yellow peppers on the same plate. Offer the Mediterranean tomato salad separately.

Rabbit, an often-overlooked delicacy, tastes somewhat like chicken. Because its flesh is lean and delicate, rabbit is enhanced by marinating, as in this recipe. Do not cook rabbit directly over hot coals: Use a covered barbecue for indirect cooking and lay the rabbit pieces at the perimeter of the fire. Otherwise, the meat will dry out.

What to drink
These vivid, summery flavours interact well with a full-flavoured dry red wine such as a Chianti Classico, a Gigondas, or even a Châteauneuf-du-Pape.

Start-to-Finish Steps
1 Start barbecue, using masquite, if available.
2 Follow rabbit recipe steps 1 through 3.
3 Follow peppers recipe steps 1 and 2.
4 Follow salad recipe steps 1 through 3.
5 Follow peppers recipe steps 3 and 4.
6 After 10 minutes, follow rabbit recipe step 4.
7 After 5 minutes, follow rabbit recipe step 5.
8 Follow peppers recipe steps 5 through 8.
9 Follow salad recipe step 4, rabbit recipe step 6, peppers recipe step 9, and serve.

Grilled Rabbit

6 cloves garlic
3 small hot red or green chili peppers, or 1 teaspoon
    hot red pepper flakes
350 ml (12 fl oz) soy sauce
350 ml (12 fl oz) dry red wine
250 ml (8 fl oz) red wine vinegar
6 branches fresh thyme, or 1 teaspoon dried
2 bay leaves
Two 1.5–2 Kg (2^1/$_2$–3 lb) rabbits, each cut into 6
pieces

1 Peel and halve garlic.
2 Wearing rubber gloves, wash fresh chilies, if using.
    Pat dry with paper towels, stem, and chop coarsley.
3 In large glass or enamel-lined baking dish, combine
    garlic and chilies, or dried red pepper flakes, with
    soy sauce, wine, vinegar, thyme, and bay leaves.
    Add rabbit and marinate 15 minutes, turning
    occasionally.
4 With slotted spoon, transfer rabbit to centre of grill.
    Reserve marinade. Cover barbecue and, with vent
    open, cook rabbit 20 to 30 minutes.
5 Transfer marinade to small enamel-lined saucepan.
    On grill, reduce 15 to 20 minutes, or until slightly
    thickened.
6 With tongs, divide rabbit among individual dinner
    plates and spoon reduced marinade over rabbit.

Grilled Yellow and Green Bell Peppers

6 cloves garlic
2 yellow bell peppers
2 green bell peppers
4 tablespoons olive oil
Salt and freshly ground black pepper

1 Peel and mince garlic, and transfer to small bowl.
2 Wash peppers and pat dry with paper towels.
3 When coals are covered by white ash, using rake,
    move coals to sides of barbecue, leaving space in
    centre. Place grill 4 inches from coals and heat 3
    to 4 minutes.
4 Place peppers around edge of grill and cook 20 to
    30 minutes, turning often with tongs to make sure
    peppers char evenly. Yellow peppers will take
    about 5 minutes longer than green peppers.
5 Place peppers in paper bag, and roll up top to seal
    tightly. Let sit until cooled and moist, about 10
    minutes.

6 Remove peppers from bag and rub gently with
    paper towel to remove charred skin.
7 For dressing, combine olive oil with garlic.
8 Core, quarter, and seed peppers.
9 Arrange peppers alongside rabbit, alternating
    yellow and green pieces. Spoon dressing over top,
    and season with salt and pepper to taste.

Mediterranean Tomato Salad

Large bunch watercress
2 tablespoons coarsely chopped fresh basil,
    preferably, or oregano, chervil, cilantro, or parsley
500 g (1 lb) firm ripe tomatoes
60 g (2 oz) niçoise, Greek, or oil-cured black olives
60 g (2 oz) feta cheese, preferably Bulgarian,
    crumbled
3 tablespoons red wine vinegar
6 tablespoons plus 2 tablespoons olive oil

1 Keeping watercress and basil or other herbs separate
    remove stems, wash, and dry in salad spinner or
    pat dry with paper towels. Divide watercress
    among 4 salad plates. Reserve basil.
2 Wash tomatoes and pat dry. Core tomatoes and cut
    into 1 cm (^{1}/$_2$ inch) slices. Arrange slices on top of
    watercress.
3 Distribute olives and feta over tomato slices. Set
    aside and keep cool.
4 In small bowl, combine basil, vinegar, and olive
    oil, stirring with fork until blended. Spoon dressing
    over salad.

Pork Loin Roasted with Garlic and Sage
Artichokes Oreganata
Tapénade

When you serve this elegant picnic, arrange the pork loin slices and the artichokes on separate platters. Offer the tapénade in a pitcher with a spoon for ladling and serve the bread in a napkin-lined basket.

You can serve this meal as a picnic or as a barbecue, since the boneless pork roast can be either roasted or barbecued. If you cook the pork in the oven, slice it after it cools and then take it to your picnic wrapped in plastic or foil. For a barbecue, grill the pork just before mealtime, so it comes to the table hot.

The tapénade is a classic Provençale purée of black olives, garlic, anchovies, and capers. It is an integral part of this meal and should be served both as a sauce for the pork and as a dip for the artichokes. Tapénade can be made in advance and refigerated for up to two weeks.

What to drink

It is difficult to choose a wine to accompany artichokes, but the other dishes in this menu go well with a full-bodied white wine or a relatively light red. For the white, try a white Châteauneuf-du-Pape or a Mâcon; for the red, Italian Valpolicella or Bardolino.

Start-to-Finish Steps

Thirty minutes ahead: If using barbecue, start fire, using mesquite, if available.

1 Follow pork recipe steps 1 through 6.
2 While pork is cooking, follow artichoke recipe steps 1 through 4.
3 While artichokes are cooking, follow tapénade recipe step 1.
4 Follow artichokes recipe steps 5 and 6.
5 While artichokes are cooling, follow pork recipe step 7.
6 Follow pork recipe step 8.
7 Follow tapénade recipe steps 2 through 3 and artichokes recipe step 7. Slice bread and place in basket.
8 Follow pork recipe step 9 and serve with artichokes, tapénade, and bread.

Pork Loin Roasted with Garlic and Sage

1 lemon
1.25 Kg (2¹/₂ lb) pork loin, boned, rolled, and tied
Salt and freshly ground black pepper
5 fresh sage leaves, or 1 tablespoon dried rubbed
    sage, plus sage sprigs for garnish (optional)
4 cloves garlic
Tapénade (see following recipe)

1 If not using barbecue, preheat oven to 240°C (475°F or Mark 9).
2 Halve lemon. Squeeze one half over pork and rub meat with juice.
3 Sprinkle pork with salt and pepper to taste and with dried sage, if using, and pat lightly to make grains adhere.
4 Peel and sliver garlic. Arrange garlic on top of pork in 2 lengthwise rows. If using fresh sage, wash, pat dry with paper towels, and place end to end, between rows of garlic.
5 If barbecuing, move coals with barbecue rake to one side, leaving space in centre. Place grill 10 cm (4 inches) from coals and heat 2 to 3 minutes.
6 If barbecuing, place pork in centre of grill, not over coals. Cover barbecue, open vents in lid, and cook pork 50 to 60 minutes. If not barbecuing, lay pork on rack in roasting pan and place in oven. Cook 10 minutes, lower oven temperature to 190°C (375°F or Mark 5) and cook 40 to 50 minutes more.
7 Slice remaining lemon half for garnish, if desired.
8 Remove pork from barbecue or oven and, if serving warm, let rest 10 minutes.
9 When ready to serve, cut pork into 1–2 cm (¹/₂-³/₄ inch) slices. Arrange slices on platter, garnish with lemon slices and sage sprigs, if desired, and serve with tapénade.

Artichokes Oreganata

4 medium-size globe artichokes
2 branches fresh oregano, or 1 teaspoon dried
1 lemon
4 cloves garlic
2 tablespoons olive oil
2 teaspoons salt
Basil sprigs for garnish (optional)
Tapénade (see following recipe)

1 In large covered saucepan, bring 2¹/₂ ltrs (4 pts) water to a boil over high heat.
2 Carefully spreading leaves apart, wash artichokes thoroughly under cold running water. Drain, and with very sharp paring knife, trim stems and prickly ends of leaves.
3 If using fresh oregano, remove stems and wash. With chef's knife, halve lemon and unpeeled garlic cloves. add one lemon half, garlic, fresh or dried oregano, olive oil, and salt to boiling water.
4 Add artichokes to boiling water. Moisten folded clean kitchen towel and place on top of artichokes, cover saucepan, reduce heat, and simmer until point of knife easily penetrates base of artichoke, about 25 minutes.
5 With slotted spoon, transfer artichokes to colander and set upside down to drain. Let sit at least 20 minutes.
6 Slice remaining lemon half and, if using basil sprigs for garnish, wash and pat dry.
7 Arrange artichokes on platter, garnish with lemon slices and basil sprigs, if desired, and serve with tapénade.

Tapénade

250 g (8 oz) oil-cured black olives
3 tablespoons capers
6 anchovy fillets
Small bunch fresh basil
4 to 6 cloves garlic, approximately
2 lemons
150 ml (5 fl oz) olive oil
1 loaf French bread

1 With paring knife, pit olives. In strainer, rinse capers and anchovies, drain, and pat dry with paper towels. In colander, wash basil and pat dry with paper towels. Remove stems and discard. With chef's knife, coarsely chop 30 g (1 oz) leaves. Peel garlic and juice lemons.
2 In bowl of food processor or blender, combine olive oil, olives, capers, anchovies, basil, garlic, and lemon juice. Purée mixture until it is thick and smooth.
3 Using rubber spatula, transfer tapénade to sauce bowl. Garnish with basil sprig, if desired, and serve with bread.

Bruce Cliborne

Menu 1

(*left*)

Grilled Clams,
Oysters, and Lobsters
Herbed New Potatoes, Carrots,
and Scallions
Cucumbers and Tomatoes with Lime

Bruce Cliborne's clambake captures the essence of out-of-doors entertaining. For his Menu 1, prepare the meal on the beach to enjoy the scent of the sea mingling with the grilling oysters, clams, and lobsters – an experience at once both primitive and sophisticated. Traditional beach clambakes, devised by the early New England Indians, call for steaming an assortment of shellfish in a bed of seaweed over hot stones. For his version, Bruce Cliborne cooks both seafood and foil-wrapped vegetables over a wood fire. Of course, the grilled seafood is just as delicious prepared in your backyard.

Menus 2 and 3, both sumptuous picnics, are ideal for backyards or terraces but are easily transportable to some away-from-home site. Bruce Cliborne intends the fragrant thyme that scents the pork of menu 2 to evoke images of flower-filled meadows. Menu 3 consists of poached scallops on a wreath of radicchio leaves, braised fennel, and a delicately seasoned orange and radish salad.

All three menus combine seasonal choices with abundant contrasting textures, colours, and flavours. This approach to meal planning is in keeping with Bruce Cliborne's art training. As art students learn classic techniques, he believes, so cooks should master the skills of fine chefs: 'Making good food should be challenging, intriguing, amusing, and hard work,' he says.

Grilled clams, oysters, and lobsters – a variation of the traditional New England clambake – constitute an impressive main course for this barbecue. Arrange the potatoes, carrots, and scallions on a serving platter, and serve the cucumber and tomato salad in a separate bowl. Each guest will need a ramekin of saffron-butter sauce for dunking the shellfish.

Menu 1

Grilled Clams, Oysters, and Lobsters
Herbed New Potatoes, Carrots, and Scallions
Cucumbers and Tomatoes with Lime

For Bruce Cliborne's clamcake, the lobsters, clams, and oysters are grilled over wood. You can bring your own portable barbecue or, as the cook recommends, construct a pit grill at the beach, but this requires some advance preparation. For a pit grill, use the rack from your own barbecue or construct one at home: Make a grill rack by nailing four 60 x 5 x 2½ cm (24 x 2 x 1 inch) pieces of wood together. Over this frame, stretch 5 mm (¼ inch) heavy-duty mesh wire and, with a staple gun, staple it to the frame at each corner. For the fire, dig a shallow sand pit 30 cm (12 inch) deep and slightly less than 60 cm (24 inches) square. Lay the wood in the pit, and ignite it by using crumpled paper, kindling, or firestarter. Once the fire has started, lay the mesh frame over the pit. Of course, if you do not live near a beach, you may prepare this clambake over a barbecue in your own backyard.

What to drink
The lobster deserves a first-rate dry white wine with full flavour and body. Try a Chardonnay from California, a good white Burgundy from a named village, or a white Mercurey.

Start-to-Finish Steps
1   Start barbecue, using masquite, if available.
2   Follow potatoes recipe steps 1 through 4.
3   Follow cucumbers recipe steps 1 through 5.
4   Follow clams recipe steps 1 through 3.
5   Follow potatoes recipe steps 5.
6   Follow clams recipe steps 4 through 8.
7   Follow potatoes recipe step 6.
8   Follow clams recipe steps 9 through 12 and potatoes recipe step 7.
9   Follow cucumbers recipe step 6, potatoes recipe step 8, clams recipe step 13, and serve.

Grilled Clams, Oysters, and Lobsters

12 clams
12 oysters
2 large shallots
2 medium-size live lobsters (625 g (1¼ lb) each), with claws pegged or bound
250 ml (8 fl oz) dry white wine

6 leaves fresh basil, chopped
Pinch of saffron threads
250 g (8 oz) unsalted butter
Salt and freshly ground pepper

1   With wire brush, scrub clams and oysters thoroughly, and rinse in several changes of cold water.
2   Peel shallots and chop enough to measure 1 tablespoon.
3   Set sieve over small saucepan. Using oyster knife, open oysters over sieve, and pour liquor through sieve into pan. Loosen oysters from shell bottoms and discard bottoms. On aluminium foil, set aside oysters in half shells.

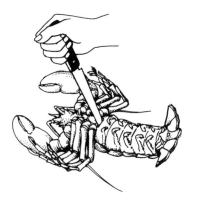

4   To kill lobsters, place them belly-up with claws still pegged or bound. While gripping lobster securely through folded towel with one hand, sever spinal cord with the other by plunging tip of knife crosswise into lobster at point where body section and tail section meet (involuntary muscle spasms may continue after lobster is dead).
5   When fire is ready, place lobsters on grill set 8 inches from heat and cook 7 to 8 minutes.
6   For sauce, bring oyster liquor to a boil over high heat. Add wine and shallots, and reduce, stirring occasionally, until about 3 tablespoons remain, about 15 minutes.
7   While sauce is reducing, chop basil.
8   Grill oysters and clams until edges of oysters have curled and clams have opened, 10 to 12 minutes.
9   Turn lobsters and cook until bright red, 4 to 7 minutes.
10 Rub saffron threads between thumb and forefinger

44

and add to sauce. Reduce heat to low.

11 Cut butter into 1-tablespoon pieces. Add butter to sauce, 1 tablespoon at a time, stirring until thoroughly incorporated. Add salt and pepper to taste.

12 Transfer lobsters, oysters, and clams to serving trays or platter and crack lobsters with nutcracker.

13 Add basil to saffron-butter sauce and divide sauce among individual ramekins. Serve sauce alongside shellfish.

Herbed New Potatoes, Carrots, and Scallions

16 small new potatoes (about 1 Kg (2 lb) total weight)
12 baby finger carrots (about 250 g (8 oz) total weight)
9 scallions, or 18 pearl onions
125 ml (4 fl oz) virgin olive oil
1 tablespoon minced fresh sage, rosemary, or thyme

1 In colander, rinse and drain potatoes, carrots, and scallions. Pat dry with paper towels.

2 With vegetable peeler, peel carrots. Trim scallions, removing roots and all but 5 cm (2 inches) of green, or peel onions, if using.

3 In large bowl, combine carrots, scallions, and potatoes. Drizzle with olive oil and toss until evenly coated. Sprinkle with sage, rosemary, or thyme and toss again.

4 Cut four 30 cm (12 inch) squares of aluminium foil and divide carrots and potatoes evenly among them. With slotted spoon, transfer carrots and potatoes to lower half of foil, arranging them in a single layer. Fold down top half of square, being careful not to disturb vegetables, and crimp edges of foil to seal. Reserve remaining oil in bowl.

5 Place packets on grill and cook 15 minutes without turning.

6 With tongs or metal spatula, carefully remove packets from grill. Open packets and add scallions or onions next to, not on top of, carrots and potatoes. If desired, add remaining oil from bowl. Reseal packets and return to grill, turning packets so 'uncooked' side is down. Cook 15 minutes.

7 Remove packets from grill and leave sealed until ready to serve.

8 Open packets and turn vegetables into serving bowl.

Cucumbers and Tomatoes with Lime

3 medium-size tomatoes or 6 Italian plum tomatoes (about 350 g (12 oz) total weight)
4 medium-size cucumbers (about 1 Kg (2 lb) total weight)
2 cloves garlic
2 small limes
4 tablespoons virgin olive oil
2 tablespoons white wine vinegar or tarragon vinegar
1 tablespoon chopped fresh chives
1 tablespoon chopped fresh basil, plus additional sprigs for garnish (optional)
Salt and freshly ground pepper

1 Wash tomatoes and pat dry with paper towels. With chef's knife, cut tomatoes into 5 mm (1/4 inch) slices. Transfer to large bowl.

2 With vegetable peeler, peel cucumbers. Halve cucumbers lengthwise and, with teaspoon, scoop out seeds and discard.

3 Lay cucumbers cut side down and slice into 5 mm (1/4 inch) crescents. Add to bowl with tomatoes.

4 Peel and mince garlic. Squeeze 4 tablespoons lime juice.

5 In small bowl, combine garlic, lime juice, olive oil, vinegar, chives, basil, and salt and pepper to taste. Beat with fork until blended.

6 Pour dressing over salad and toss gently until evenly coated. Garnish with basil sprigs, if desired.

Menu 2

Grilled Loin of Pork with Fresh Thyme
Marinated Corn Salad
Sweet-and-Sour Peaches and Plums

For this elegant picnic, serve the pork and vegetables at room temperature, and the fruit cooled.

Grill the slices of pork loin in a cast-iron grilling pan, a versatile piece of equipment that cooks meat and fish quickly with relatively little oil or fat. These pans, which resemble corrugated or ridged frying pans, sit directly on the flame. For this recipe, brush the ridged surface with olive oil, then lay sprigs of fresh thyme on the ridges before adding the pork slices. If you do not own this kind of pan, use a heavy-gauge skillet instead.

Thyme is a highly aromatic woody perennial that grows relatively easily in sunny garden plots. Its tiny leaves contain various powerful oils that make them pungent and flavourful even when dried. Fresh thyme may be available from speciality food stores or from certain greengrocers.

For the last course, peaches and plums are poached in wine and balsamic vinegar, a mellow, slightly sweet, aged Italian vinegar. When the fruit is cooked, remove it immediately from the poaching liquid to preserve its texture.

A napkin-lined wicker basket is attractive as well as convenient for serving the sliced grilled pork loin. Large glass jars with tight-fitting lids are perfect for carrying and serving the poached fruit and the marinated salad.

What to drink

The best choice here would be beer or ale. If you prefer wine, pick a soft fruity white: a German or California Riesling, or a California French Colombard.

Start-to-Finish Steps

1 Follow peaches recipe steps 1 through 6. While liquid is simmering, chill platter for peaches.
2 Follow peaches recipe step 7.
3 While fruit is poaching, peel shallots and follow corn recipe steps 1 through 3.
4 Follow peaches recipe step 8.
5 Follow corn recipe steps 4 through 10.
6 Follow pork recipe steps 1 through 5.
7 Follow corn recipe step 11, peaches recipe step 9, and pork recipe step 6.

Grilled Loin of Pork with Fresh Thyme

3 tablespoons olive oil, approximately

12 sprigs thyme
$4^{1}/_{2}$ cm ($1^{3}/_{4}$ inch) thick centre-cut pork loin slices, boned and trimmed (about 750 g ($1^{1}/_{2}$ lbs) total weight)
Salt
Freshly ground black pepper

1 Coat bottom of grill pan with oil.
2 Heat pan over medium-high heat. Add 4 thyme sprigs. When thyme releases its fragrance, add pork slices, arranging them in single layer
3 Reduce heat to medium-low and cook pork 12 to 15 minutes. Using tongs, remove thyme sprigs as they char and replace them with fresh sprigs. If using cast-iron pan, pour off pork fat as it accumulates.
4 Using tongs, turn pork and cook until slightly browned and running juices show no trace of pink, 12 to 15 minutes. Season with salt and pepper to taste.
5 With metal spatula or tongs, transfer pork to paper towels to drain. Let cool 10 minutes.
6 Pack in foil for transporting.

Marinated Corn Salad

4 tablespoons virgin olive oil
6 large shallots (about 125 g (4 oz) total weight),
    peeled
2 medium-size red bell peppers
1 clove garlic
1/2 teaspoon black peppercorns
Salt
Freshly ground black pepper
4 ears fresh corn
1/2 teaspoon fresh thyme
1 1/2 teaspoons coarsely chopped parsley
3 tablespoons dry white wine
2 teaspoons sherry vinegar or red wine vinegar

1 In large sauté pan, heat 2 tablespoons olive oil
   over medium heat 30 seconds. Reduce heat to low,
   add shallots, and cook, stirring frequently with
   wooden spoon, until translucent and crisp-tender,
   4 to 5 minutes.
2 Wash red peppers and pat dry with paper towels.
   Halve, core, and seed peppers. Cut each half
   lengthwise into 3 sections. Peel and mince garlic.
   Crush peppercorns.
3 With slotted spoon, transfer shallots to large bowl.
4 Add red peppers to sauté pan and season with salt
   and pepper to taste. Cook in remaining oil over
   medium-low heat, stirring frequently with wooden
   spoon, until peppers are just barely tender, about
   10 minutes.
5 Trim stub end of corn so that it will rest flat on
   cutting board. Holding corn perpendicular to
   cutting board, slice downward with chef's knife,
   removing kernels. Turn over and repeat until all
   kernels are removed are removed.
6 With slotted spoon, transfer cooked peppers to
   bowl with shallots.

7 Add corn to sauté pan and cook, stirring frequently,
   until corn is tender, about 6 minutes.
8 Add garlic and crushed black peppercorns to corn
   and stir to combine.
9 With slotted spoon, transfer corn to bowl with
   shallots and peppers. Add thyme, parsley, white
   wine, and vinegar and stir to combine.
10 Let mixture cool to room temperature, stirring
   frequently.
11 Pack cooled mixture into jar with tight-fitting lid or
   other suitable container.

Sweet-and-Sour Peaches and Plums

Medium-size orange
2 medium-size lemons
4 large barely ripe peaches
8 large firm plums
4 pears (if peaches or plums are unavailable)
60 g (2 oz) golden raisins
60 g (2 oz) brown sugar
1 tablespoon balsamic vinegar or red wine vinegar
2 whole cloves
500 ml (16 fl oz) red wine, preferably Burgundy

1 In large saucepan, bring 3 ltrs (5 pts) water to a boil
   over high heat.
2 Fill large bowl with ice water. Strip zest from 1/2
   orange and cut zest into julienne strips. Juice
   lemons.
3 Add peaches and plums, or pears, if using, to
   boiling water and blanch about 30 seconds.
4 With slotted spoon, gently but rapidly transfer fruit
   to bowl of ice water and let sit 1 minute. Transfer
   fruit to colander and drain.
5 With paring knife or fingers, peel fruit, being
   careful not to pierce flesh.
6 In saucepan, combine raisins, lemon juice, brown
   sugar, vinegar, orange zest, cloves, and red wine.
   Bring to a simmer over medium-high heat, and
   cook 5 minutes.
7 Add fruit and simmer gently, removing each piece
   of fruit when barely tender, 3 to 6 minutes for
   plums, 4 to 8 minutes for peaches, and 13 to 18
   minutes for pears, if using.
8 With slotted spoon, transfer fruit to chilled platter
   and transfer poaching syrup to chilled small bowl
   or jar with metal spoon in it to absorb heat. Let cool
   to room temperature, 30 to 45 minutes. Refrigerate,
   if desired.
9 When ready to leave for picnic, recombine fruit
   and syrup in jar with tight-fitting lid or other
   suitable container.

Added touch

The artichokes are filled with a savoury stuffing of prosciutto (an Italian ham) and either wild or shiitake mushrooms. Fresh cultivated mushrooms will also do.

Artichokes Stuffed with Wild Mushrooms and Prosciutto

Salt
4 medium-size to large artichokes
3 medium-size lemons
250 g (8 oz) thinly sliced prosciutto
250 g (8 oz) wild Black Forest, shiitake, or golden oak
   mushrooms, preferably, or fresh cultivated
   mushrooms
2 medium-size red bell peppers
175 ml (6 fl oz) olive oil
1/2 teaspoon chopped thyme
1/2 teaspoon chopped oregano
3 cloves garlic
4 tablespoons red wine vinegar
1/2 teaspoon chopped parsley
Freshly ground black pepper

1 In large saucepan, bring 4 ltrs (7 pts) water and 4 teaspoons salt to a boil over high heat.

2 Holding artichokes under cold running water, gently force leaves apart and rinse thoroughly. Trim off stems and any wilted or browned leaves.

3 Add artichokes to boiling water and reduce to a simmer. Juice lemons and add juice and rinds to pan. Fold a clean dishcloth in half, wet it, and place directly on top of artichokes to keep them moist as they float to surface.

4 Cook artichokes at a simmer just until point of knife easily penetrates base and leaves pull off with little resistance, 30 to 45 minutes.

5 Fill large bowl with iced water. With slotted spoon, rapidly transfer artichokes to iced water. Leave 1 minute and transfer to colander.

6 When cool enough to handle, part centre leaves of each artichoke with your fingers. Using teaspoon, if necessary, remove innermost leaves and centre spikes just above the heart. Set artichokes upside down on paper towels to drain.

7 With chef's knife, slice prosciutto into 5 mm (1/4 inch) julienne strips. Wipe mushrooms with damp paper towels and cut into 5 mm (1/4 inch) slices. Wash peppers and pat dry with paper towels. Halve, core, and seed peppers. Cut each half into 5 mm (1/4 inch) strips.

8 In medium-sized skillet, heat 2 tablespoons olive oil over medium heat about 30 seconds. Add prosciutto and sauté, stirring frequently with wooden spoon, until strips stiffen and crisp slightly, 3 to 4 minutes. Drizzle in more olive oil, if necessary, to prevent sticking. With slotted spoon, transfer prosciutto to large bowl.

9 Add 2 tablespoons olive oil to skillet and heat 30 seconds. Add mushrooms and sauté, stirring frequently, until mushrooms are lightly browned, 7 to 10 minutes. With slotted spoon, transfer mushrooms to bowl.

10 Add 2 tablespoons olive oil to skillet and heat 30 seconds. Add red pepper strips and sauté over medium heat until crisp-tender, about 4 minutes. With slotted spoon, transfer peppers to bowl.

11 Add thyme and oregano to prosciutto mixture and toss to combine.

12 Turn artichokes right side up. With teaspoon, stuff centre of artichokes with equal amounts of mixture and set aside.

13 Peel and mince garlic.

14 In medium-size jar with tight-fitting lid, combine remaining olive oil, vinegar, garlic, parsley, and pepper to taste. Shake dressing until blended and spoon over each artichoke just before serving.

Sea Scallops with Herbed Crème Fraîche
Poached Fennel
Orange, Radish, and Coriander Salad

Serve the sliced sea scallops on a bed of radicchio leaves and garnish them with mint. The poached fennel or celery and the orange-red salad require individual bowls. If you wish, offer a basket of fresh bread with the meal.

Prepare this picnic far enough in advance to allow all its components to chill thoroughly.

Sea scallops, unlike the smaller bay scallops, are available fresh most of the year and are sold frozen as well. For this menu, scallops are served with *crème fraîche*, a French cultured-cream product resembling sour cream. Not many supermarkets stock *crème fraîche*, but you can easily make your own in advance.

What to drink
Try an Alsatian or California Gewürztramminer to complement the spiciness of the menu.

Start-to-Finish Steps
1 Follow fennel recipe steps 1 through 3.
2 While fennel is poaching, follow scallops recipe steps 1 through 4.
3 Follow salad recipe step 1.
4 Follow fennel recipe step 4 and scallops recipe steps 5 through 9.
5 Follow salad recipe steps 2 and 3, and scallops recipe step 10.
6 Follow scallops recipe step 11 and salad recipe step 4.
7 Follow scallops recipe step 12, salad recipe step 5, fennel recipe step 5, and serve or pack up picnic.

Sea Scallops with Herbed Crème Fraîche

Medium-size Spanish onion
2 medium-size carrots
1 lemon
3 star anise
1 teaspoon green peppercorns
2 bay leaves
2 heads radicchio or Boston lettuce
250 ml (8 fl oz) dry white wine
750 g (1½ lb) sea scallops
250 ml (8 fl oz) crème fraîche, well chilled
1 tablespoon chopped mint
1 tablespoon chopped basil
Salt

1 Peel onion and carrots, and cut into 2½ mm (⅛ inch) slices.
2 Strip zest from lemon.

3 In stainless steel skillet, combine 500 ml (1 pt) cold water, onion, carrots, lemon zest, star anise, green peppercorns, and bay leaves. Cover, bring to a boil over medium-high heat, and simmer, partially covered, 20 minutes.

4 Wash radicchio and dry in salad spinner or pat dry with paper towels. Set platter in refrigerator to chill.

5 Add wine to poaching liquid and simmer 5 minutes.

6 Wipe scallops with damp paper towels. With chef's knife, halve each scallop.

7 Pour poaching liquid through sieve set over large bowl. Return sieved liquid to skillet and return to a simmer over medium-high heat. Rinse out bowl.

8 Add scallops and poach 2 to 3 minutes.

9 With slotted spoon, transfer scallops to chilled platter and refrigerate 10 minutes.

10 In cleaned bowl, combine crème fraîche and herbs.

11 Add chilled scallops to crème fraîche mixture and toss gently to combine. Add salt to taste and toss again.

12 In large carrying container with lid or in serving dish, arrange radicchio or lettuce leaves in a wreath. Spoon scallops into centre of wreath.

Poached Fennel

1 clove garlic, peeled and minced
500 ml (1 pt) chicken stock
250 ml (8 fl oz) dry white wine
2 bay leaves
Salt and freshly ground pepper
4 fennel bulbs or 4 hearts of celery
1 tablespoon chopped parsley

1 In medium-size stainless steel sauté pan, combine garlic, stock, wine, bay leaves, and salt and pepper to taste. Bring to a boil over medium-high heat.

2 With chef's knife, trim fennel, leaving about 15 cm (6 inches) of stalk, and remove nubbin at bottom of bulb. Rinse bulb under cold water and pat dry with paper towels. Quarter bulb lengthwise.

3 Add fennel to pan, lower heat, and simmer until barely tender when pierced with knife, 20 to 30 minutes.

4 With slotted spoon, transfer fennel to serving platter or to carrying container and cool at least 20 minutes.

5 Before serving or packing, sprinkle fennel or celery with parsley.

Orange, Radish, and Coriander Salad

8 medium-size seedless oranges
Large red onion, peeled and sliced
Small bunch radishes (6 to 8), washed and trimmed
125 ml (4 fl oz) virgin olive oil
6 tablespoons red wine vinegar or tarragon vinegar
1 teaspoon Szechwan peppercorns or black peppercorns
1 tablespoon coriander seeds
Salt and freshly ground pepper

1 With paring knife, trim peel and white pith from oranges. Then, over medium-size bowl or deep carrying container with lid, holding orange in one hand and knife in other, free segments by cutting toward centre on each side of membranes, letting segments fall into bowl.

2 Separate onion into rings and add to oranges.

3 Coarsely grate radishes into bowl with orange mixture. Using wooden spoon, toss gently to combine.

4 In small bowl, combine oil, vinegar, peppercorns, coriander seeds, and salt and pepper to taste.

5 Pour dressing over salad and toss gently but thoroughly until salad is well-coated with dressing.

Nicholas Baxter

Menu 1
(*Right*)
Loin of Lamb with Tomato and
Mushroom Stuffing
Watercress and Hazelnut Salad
Pasta with Sour Cream
and Black Pepper

Nicholas Baxter has a straightforward culinary maxim: A glorious meal does not require a multitude of ingredients and lengthy preparation. Quality components, carefully arranged on the dinner plate, will please both the palate and the eye. 'If the meal does not form an alluring still life on the plate,' he says, 'guests do not quickly discover that it tastes good.'

When he plans a meal, he makes one course spectacular and downplays the rest. This way, the diners' taste buds are not overwhelmed. For Menu 1, the focal point is barbecued lamb, a delicious alternative to grilled beef. Stuffed with a flavourful chopped tomato mixture, which provides a textural contrast, the lamb is served with a watercress and hazelnut salad, and pasta with sour cream.

The grilled salmon steaks in Menu 2 are the centrepiece, accompanied by mixed spring vegetables. The loin of veal in Menu 3 is poached in a stock based on Alsatian Riesling, which the chef calls the nearest thing to fresh grapes in wine form.

Garnish the barbecued loin of lamb with lettuce leaves and tomato wedges, and serve it on a platter. Sprinkle the pasta with fresh snipped chives. The watercress salad is easy to carry in a covered serving dish.

Loin of Lamb with Tomato and Mushroom Stuffing
Watercress and Hazelnut Salad
Pasta with Sour Cream and Black Pepper

Cook this backyard barbecue in stages: Complete the salad and pasta indoors in the intervals between basting the lamb outdoors.

The loin, the tenderest cut of lamb, is filled with a tomato and mushroom stuffing and then tied up with string. Ask your butcher to bone the loin and to cut an envelope for the stuffing between the top layer of fat and the meat. You can oven-roast the lamb, but it tastes best barbecued.

Watercress is available at most supermarkets and greengrocers year round.. The leaves should be crisp and green and have no sign of wilt or discoloration. Rinse watercress in cold water, pat it dry with paper towels, and refrigerate the bunch in a plastic bag, where it will keep for a week. If you wish, you can use dandelion greens or arugula instead. Hazelnuts, are slightly sweet and less oily than pecans. They are sold in bulk at speciality food shops and many health food stores. If not available, you can use slivered almonds instead.

What to drink
Grilled lamb with garlic calls for a dry red wine; try a California Cabernet Sauvignon, a claret from the Médoc, or a Bordeaux village wine, such as a St. Julien or Margaux.

Start-to-Finish Steps

Thirty minutes ahead: Start barbecue and place rack 10 cm (4 inches) from coals.

1 Follow stuffing recipe steps 1 through 7.
2 Follow lamb recipe steps 1 through 8.
3 While lamb is cooking, follow orzo recipe step 1.
4 While water is heating, follow lamb recipe step 9.
5 Follow orzo recipe step 2.
6 While orzo is cooking, follow salad recipe steps 1 through 3.
7 Follow orzo recipe steps 3 and salad recipe step 4.
8 Follow orzo recipe steps 4 and 5.
9 Follow lamb recipe step 10.
10 While meat is resting, follow orzo recipe step 6 and salad recipe step 5.
11 Carve lamb and serve with salad and orzo.

Loin of Lamb with Tomato and Mushroom Stuffing

2 cloves garlic
1.5 Kg (3 lb) loin of lamb, boned, with pocket cut lengthwise between fat and surface of meat
Tomato and Mushroom Stuffing (see following recipe)
4 tablespoons extra-virgin olive oil
1 tablespoon dried oregano
Small head Boston lettuce for garnish (optional)
Large tomato for garnish (optional)

1 Peel garlic and cut in half lengthwise.
2 With cut side of garlic, rub inside of lamb pocket, both fat and meat.
3 With garlic press, crush garlic into tomato and mushroom stuffing and stir to combine.
4 With slotted spoon, scoop up stuffing mixture, allowing each spoonful to drain slightly, and fill lamb pocket.
5 Using kitchen string, carefully tie up lamb to close the pocket, securing the stuffing inside.
6 In small bowl, combine olive oil and oregano.
7 When fire is ready, place lamb on grill 10 cm (4

inches) above coals. Using basting brush, brush lamb with oil mixture.

8   When flames from the dripping fat have subsided, lower rack to within 7½ cm (3 inches) of coals. Cook lamb, turning and basting every 8 to 10 minutes, until juices run pale pink, a total of about 40 minutes.

9   For garnish, if using, wash lettuce and dry in salad spinner or pat dry with paper towels. Wash tomato, if using, pat dry, and cut into wedges.

10 Just before meat is done, line serving platter with lettuce leaves, if using. With 2 metal spatulas or 2 barbecue forks, transfer meat to platter. Carefully remove string, and let lamb rest 5 to 10 minutes before carving.

Tomato and Mushroom Stuffing

4 medium-size tomatoes
Large Spanish onion
175 g (6 oz) mushrooms
3 tablespoons tomato purée
2 tablespoons unsalted butter
½ tablespoon salt

1   In small saucepan, bring just enough water to cover tomatoes by 1 cm (½ inch) to a boil over high heat.

2   While water is heating, with paring knife cut a cross in the top and bottom of each tomato, just penetrating skin. Peel onion and set aside. Wipe mushrooms with damp paper towels and, using paring knife, trim off 5 mm (¼ inch) of stems. Quarter mushrooms lengthwise, or, if very large, cut into eighths.

3   When water is boiling, add tomatoes and blanch 30 seconds. In colander, drain tomatoes and cool under cold running water. Peel off skins.

4   Halve, seed, and core tomatoes. Cut each half into 1 cm (½ inch) dice and place in medium-size bowl. Add tomato purée and, using wooden spoon, stir to combine. Add mushrooms and mix well.

5   In food processor, chop onion coarsely, pulsing on and off about 6 seconds. Or, with chef's knife, chop coarsely.

6   In medium-size skillet, heat butter over medium heat until just melted, about 1 minute. Do not let butter brown. Add onion to skillet and cook over medium heat, stirring occasionally with wooden spoon, 3 minutes.

7   Add tomato and mushroom mixture, and stir to combine. Season with salt, and cook over medium heat about 5 minutes, or until mixture has thickened slightly. Remove pan from heat and set aside.

Watercress and Hazelnut Salad

3 bunches watercress or 2 bunches dandelion greens (about 500 g (1 lb) total weight)
125 g (4 oz) shelled hazelnuts, preferably, or 125 g (4 oz) slivered almonds
1 lemon
2 tablespoons extra-virgin olive oil
Salt and freshly ground black pepper

1   Preheat oven to 180°C (350°F or Mark 4).

2   Wash watercress or dandelion greens and dry in salad spinner or pat dry with paper towels. Remove stems from watercress or trim dandelion stems and discard. Place greens in salad bowl, cover with plastic wrap and refrigerate until ready to serve.

3   Place hazelnuts on jelly-roll pan and toast in oven 4 to 6 minutes. If using almonds, toast 3 to 4 minutes, or until very lightly browned.

4   Remove hazelnuts from oven and allow to cool slightly. Juice lemon and strain to remove pits.

5   Spoon olive oil over watercress or dandelion greens and toss until evenly coated. Add lemon juice and toss again. Sprinkle salad with nuts and season with salt and pepper to taste.

Pasta with Sour Cream and Black Pepper

250 g (8 oz) orzo, or other small-shape pasta
Small bunch fresh chives
3 tablespoons sour cream
2 teaspoons salt
Freshly ground black pepper

1   In medium-size saucepan, bring 2½ ltrs (4 pts) water to the boil.

2   Add pasta to boiling water and simmer until tender, 9–10 minutes.

3   In colander, drain pasta and allow to cool, tossing occasionally with wooden spoon.

4   Wash chives, pat dry with paper towels, and chop enough to measure 2 tablespoons.

5   When pasta is cool, transfer to medium-size bowl. Add sour cream and, using 2 wooden spoons, toss until evenly coated. Add salt and toss again.

6   Just before serving, grind black pepper to taste over pasta and sprinkle with chives.

Menu 2

Grilled Salmon Steaks with Fresh Dill and Thyme
Mélange of French Vegetables

For this simple barbecue, grill both components of the meal, wrapped in foil packets, simultaneously. As the meal's focal point, Nicholas Baxter has selected salmon Steaks, whose firm texture makes them ideal for grilling. The vegetable packets consist of leeks, tomatoes, and courgettes. Be sure to wash the leeks carefully; sand gets trapped in the leafy tops.

What to drink

To stand alongside the rich flavour of the fish, choose either a California Sauvignon Blanc or a French Pouilly Fumé.

On individual trays, arrange the salmon garnished with dill and lemon slices and the vegetables, all in foil wrappings.

Start-to-Finish Steps

1 Start barbecue.
2 If using fresh herbs, strip thyme leaves from branches. Wash dill and basil, and pat dry with paper towels. With chef's knife, chop basil separately and then chop dill and thyme.
3 Follow vegetables recipe steps 1 through 6.
4 Follow salmon recipe steps 1 through 4.
5 When vegetables have been on grill 5 minutes, follow salmon recipe step 5.
6 Follow salmon recipe step 6, and vegetables recipe step 7, and serve.

Grilled Salmon Steaks with Fresh Dill and Thyme

2 lemons, plus additional lemon for garnish (optional)
4 salmon steaks (each about 250 g (8 oz))

3 tablespoons chopped fresh dill, or 1 tablespoon dried
3 tablespoons chopped fresh thyme, or 1 tablespoon dried, plus 4 branches for garnish (optional)
4 tablespoons unsalted butter
Salt and freshly ground pepper

1 Slice 1 lemon into wedges for garnish, if desired. Grate zest from 2 lemons.
2 With damp paper towels, wipe salmon steaks. Sprinkle both sides of steaks with dill, thyme, and lemon zest.
3 Cut four 30 cm (12 inch) square sheets of foil and place 1 salmon steak on lower half of each. Top each steak with 1 tablespoon butter.
4 Bring free half of foil over steak to form rectangle. Fold edges together and crimp to seal.
5 When grill is ready, place packets on barbecue and cook 5 minutes. Turn and cook 5 minutes on other side.
6 Transfer packets to individual basket, if desired. Open packets, season with salt and pepper to taste, and garnish with lemon wedges and a branch of thyme, if desired.

Mélange of Fresh Vegetables

8 small leeks
4 medium-size courgettes, each about 15 cm
    (6 inches) long
8 medium-size tomatoes
3 tablespoons chopped fresh basil, or 2 tablespoons
    dried
125 ml (4 fl oz) sweet apple cider
Salt and freshly ground pepper

1   In large saucepan, bring to a boil enough water to
    cover tomatoes by about 2¹/₂ cm (1 inch).
2   With chef's knife, trim greens and roots from leeks,
    and discard. Split leeks lengthwise and rinse
    thoroughly under cold running water to remove
    sand and grit.
3   Trim ends from courgettes, wash, and pat dry.
    With chef's knife, quarter each courgette lengthwise.
4   Plunge tomatoes into boiling water and blanch
    30 seconds. Transfer tomatoes to colander and
    refresh under cold running water. Peel, quarter,
    and seed tomatoes.
5   Cut four 30 cm (12 inch) sheets of aluminium foil.
    Divide vegetables equally among sheets. Sprinkle
    each portion with basil and 2 tablespoons cider.
    Fold edges of foil together and crimp to seal.
6   Place packets on barbecue and cook 15 minutes.
7   To serve, unwrap packets and season with salt and
    pepper to taste.

Added touch
Potato starch makes this cake light and airy. If
unavailable, substitute white flour in the same
proportion.

Light Chocolate Cake

60 g (2 oz) potato starch (potato flour)
60 g (2 oz) Dutch cocoa powder
6 eggs
125 g (4 oz) sugar
125 ml (4 fl oz) milk

1   Preheat oven to 170°C (325°F or Mark 3).
2   Sift together potato starch and cocoa powder.
3   Separate eggs, placing yolks in small bowl and
    whites in large bowl.
4   Using electric mixer, beat yolks until thick and
    lemon coloured, about 5 minutes. Yolks should
    form a continuous ribbon from raised beater.
    Wash and dry beaters thoroughly.
5   Beat egg whites at slow speed until they foam, 2 to
    3 minutes. Increase speed to medium and beat
    whites until they form soft peaks, about 3 minutes.
    Sprinkle in sugar, increase speed to high, and beat
    until whites are stiff but still shiny.
6   Reduce speed to low and gradually pour in yolks.
    When yolks are almost completely incorporated,
    sprinkle in cocoa powder mixture, add milk all at
    once, and beat just until blended.
7   Turn batter into ungreased 22¹/₂ x 12¹/₂ x 6 cm (9
    x 5 x 2¹/₂ inch) loaf pan.
8   Place pan on middle rack of oven and bake until
    cake tester inserted in centre comes out clean, 50 to
    60 minutes.
9   Remove pan from oven and place, upside down,
    so it is supported at ends by 2 heatproof items of
    same height. Let pan hang 10 minutes.
10 Turn cake onto rack and let cool.

Loin of Veal Poached with Vegetables in White Wine
Wild Rice with Red Pepper and Cassis

Plan this menu as a backyard picnic so you can serve the meal slightly warm. If you wish to have an away-from-home picnic, wrap each dish – first in foil, then in a layer of newspaper – to keep the meal warm until serving.

The main-dish loin of veal is poached in a broth made from chicken stock and Riesling wine. Produced in the Alsace region, Riesling is a perfect partner for delicately flavoured meats. It is dry, fruity, and fresh-tasting.

To make the savoury sauce for the veal, reduce the poaching liquid over high heat to half its original volume and add the caraway seeds to it before you set it aside to cool.

Wild rice is not a rice at all but the seeds of wild grass. Because it is always in short supply, it is expensive, but in this recipe 250 g (8 oz) serves four people. Before cooking, wild rice needs thorough rinsing to remove the excessively smoky taste. Deep burgundy-coloured *crème de cassis*, a French black currant liqueur, is stirred thoroughly into the wild rice and thinly coats the grains.

This picnic consists of sliced loin of veal served with celery and carrots and accompanied by wild rice and red pepper strips.

The veal dish calls for something completely dry and rather full-bodied. Try a California Chardonnay or a relatively simple Burgundy, like Mâcon or St. Véran.

Start-to-Finish Steps

1 Follow veal recipe steps 1 and 2.
2 While stock is heating, follow rice recipe steps 1 and 2.
3 While water is coming to a boil, follow veal recipe step 3.
4 Follow rice recipe step 3.
5 While rice is cooking, follow veal recipe step 4.
6 Follow rice recipe step 4 and veal recipe steps 5 and 6.
7 Follow rice recipe step 5 and veal recipe step 7.
8 Follow rice recipe step 6, veal recipe steps 8 and 9, and serve.

large bowl. To reduce liquid quickly, measure half back into casserole and half into medium-size saucepan. Bring both to a boil over high heat and reduce each by half, about 15 minutes. Stir $^1/_4$ teaspoon caraway seeds into each pan and set both aside to cool, about 10 minutes.

7 Stir reduced cooking liquid in casserole into reduced liquid in saucepan and season to taste with salt and pepper.
8 With slotted spoon, transfer veal to carving board. Remove string and slice veal into 5 mm ($^1/_4$ inch) thick medallions.
9 Place a few tablespoons of sauce on each plate and top with veal medallions. With slotted spoon, remove vegetables from liquid and arrange alongside veal. Serve remaining sauce separately.

Loin of Veal Poached with Vegetables in White Wine

4 stalks celery
4 pearl onions
8 baby carrots
1 bottle Alsatian Riesling
1$^1/_4$ ltrs (2 pts) chicken stock
14 black peppercorns
2 bay leaves
1.25 Kg (2$^1/_2$ lb) centre-cut veal tenderloin, boned, rolled, and tied
$^1/_2$ teaspoon caraway seeds
Salt
Freshly ground pepper

1 With chef's knife, trim celery stalks, halve, and cut into 10 cm (4 inch) strips. Peel onions and scrape carrots. Set aside.
2 In large casserole, combine wine, stock, peppercorns, bay leaves, and onions. Add veal and enough water to cover. With wooden spoon, stir liquid and seasonings, and bring to a simmer over high heat.
3 Lower heat to maintain a very gentle simmer, cover partially, and cook 20 minutes.
4 Add celery and carrots, partially cover pan, and continue to simmer for about 10 minutes.
5 With double-pronged fork and slotted spoon, transfer veal and vegetables to medium-size bowl. Discard onions and bay leaves. Add 500 ml (1 pt) cooking liquid to bowl with veal and vegetables, and leave uncovered to cool, 15 to 20 minutes.
6 For sauce, transfer remaining cooking liquid to

Wild Rice with Red Pepper and Cassis

250 g (8 oz) wild rice
Large red bell pepper
3 tablespoons crème de cassis

1 In sieve, rinse rice thoroughly under cold running water.
2 In medium-size saucepan, bring 500 ml (1 pt) water to rapid boil over high heat.
3 Add rice to boiling water and, with wooden spoon, stir once. Reduce to a simmer, cover and cook until tender but still slightly *al dente*, 40 minutes.
4 Wash red pepper and pat dry with paper towels. With chef's knife, halve, core, and seed pepper. Slice into 5 mm ($^1/_4$ inch) strips.
5 Drain rice in sieve and let stand 10 minutes, tossing gently with fork every 2 or 3 minutes.
6 While rice is still warm, transfer to medium-size. Add peppers and cassis, and stir gently to combine.

Meet the Cooks

Jane Uetz

Jane Uetz began her cookery career in the test kitchens of a major food company in New York City. She is the director of the consumer and culinary centre of a New York public relations agency. She also teaches cookery classes for business executives.

Roberta Rall

Roberta Rall works as a freelance food stylist and home economist. She prepares and styles food for photography for numerous publications; develops recipes for specific food products and audiences; and organizes taste tests.

Ron Davis

For three generations, Ron Davis' family have been professional cooks, so he comes by his love of cooking naturally. In 1978, he moved from Pennsylvania to New York and is now co-owner of the Washington Street Cafe as well as the Washington Street Cafe Caterers, both in New York City.

Victoria Wise

Victoria Wise, a self-taught cook, has been cooking professionally since 1971, when she left her graduate studies in philosophy to become the first chef at Berkeley's Chez Panisse, a restaurant well known to US gastronomes. She left Chez Panisse in 1973 to start her own charcuterie, called Pig by the Tail Charcuterie, in Berkeley, California.

Bruce Cliborne

Chef, food stylist, recipe developer, and caterer Bruce Cliborne experiments with elements of every kind of cuisine. Bruce Cliborne was a contributing author of and food stylist for the *Soho Charcuterie Cookbook*.

Nicholas Baxter

The son of an English diplomat, Nicholas Baxter describes himself as a restauranteur-caterer by instinct. After studying finance, he later apprenticed at the Café Royal in London. Then, he worked as a waiter, mâitre d', and manager of various restaurants in London and the Caribbean. He now owns his own catering firm.

A Wealth of Herbs

Increasingly, herbs are arriving in the markets fresh; the proliferation of health stores and other specialist shops has widened choice, and many cooks with gardens have taken to raising their own. Recent ethnic influences have called attention to once seemingly esoteric herbs. Coriander, for one, is at last gaining deserved popularity in Europe, although cooks in Asia and the Middle East have been using it for centuries.

Anyone wishing to dry fresh herbs can tie them loosely in a bundle and hang them upside down in a cool, dark, well-ventilated place for several weeks. When the leaves are completely dried, strip them from the stems and store them in an airtight container.

Two swifter methods of preserving herbs make use of the microwave oven and the freezer. To microwave herbs, place five or six sprigs at a time between paper towels and microwave them on high for 1 to 3 minutes until the leaves are brittle. Store the leaves loosely in airtight jars.

To freeze herbs, rinse the sprigs and pat them dry. Strip the leaves off the stems and put them into a heavy-duty plastic bag. Gently flatten the bag to force out the air, seal the bag tightly, and place it in your freezer. Use the leaves as the need arises.

Basil (also called sweet basil): This fragrant herb, with its underlying flavour of anise and hint of clove, goes particularly well with tomato.

Chervil: The small, lacy leaves of this herb have a taste akin to parsley with a touch of anise. It is good in salads and salad dressings. Chervil is popular in France, where it is often an ingredient in herb mixtures, including *fines herbes*. When used in cooking, chervil should be added at the end, lest its subtle flavour be lost.

Chives: The smallest of the onions, chives grow in grassy clumps. When finely cut, the hollow leaves contribute their delicate, oniony flavour to fresh salads and raw vegetables. Chives should always be used fresh, as dried ones are virtually tasteless.

Coriander (also called cilantro): The serrated leaves of the coriander plant impart a distinctive fragrance and a flavour that is both mildly sweet and bitter. Coriander leaves should be used fresh or added at the end of cooking if their flavour is to be appreciated fully.

Dill: A sprightly herb with feathery leaves, dill enhances cucumber and many other fresh vegetables, as well as fish and shellfish. When used in cooking, dill should be added towards the end of the process to preserve its delicate flavour. Both dill seeds and dill leaves can be